Jené Stonesifer

When Baby Makes Two:

❧

Single Mothers by Chance or by Choice

Lowell House
Los Angeles
Contemporary Books
Chicago

Library of Congress Cataloging-in-Publication Data
    Stonesifer, Jené.
    When baby makes two : single mothers by chance or by choice / Jené Stonesifer.
       p.   cm.
    Includes bibliographical references.
    ISBN 1-56565-158-8
    1. Unmarried mothers.   2. Single mothers.   3. Mother and child.
    I. Title.
    HQ759.45.S76   1994
    306.85'6—dc20   94-23329
                                                                CIP

Requests for such permissions should be addressed to:

Lowell House
2029 Century Park East, Suite 3290
Los Angeles, California 90067

Publisher: Jack Artenstein
General Manager, Lowell House Adult: Bud Sperry
Director of Publishing Services: Mary D. Aarons
Text Design: Janet Brandt/Frank Loose Design
Manufactured in the United States of America
10 9 8 7 6 5 4 3 2 1

To My Daughter

Acknowledgments

I am grateful to the many single mothers who took the time to divulge their innermost thoughts, speak candidly and sacrifice their privacy about their solo flights into parenthood. Each story proved unique and moving. I was constantly amazed and touched by their honesty and generosity.

These pages would not hold nearly the same value without the insight and direction of the many lawyers, judges, mediators, counselors and medical personnel I consulted. I am especially grateful to family law attorney and American Bar Association member Michael E. Barber.

I must thank Priscilla Tudela, who had faith enough in me to suggest this book. Along the way, I received constant guidance from Leah Keating, who kept our support group going and growing. I would also like to thank Patricia Cervini for the many memos, faxes and related books sent my way.

The book could not have been possible without the editing help of Michael Stuntz, a wordsmith extraordinaire; and the devotion, hard work and relentlessly long hours put in during the final stretch by Kenneth Jaques. I'm thankful also for your critiques support, Donnie Radcliffe, Robert B. McCormick and Michelle Vaughen.

As a single mother, I could not have undertaken this challenge had it not been for the generosity and cooperation of my parents—cooperation which entailed numerous hours of babysitting and the unfortunate inheritance of numerous piles of reference clutter, which spilled over from my home into theirs.

I cannot close without mention of my daughter, who, in her wisdom, patience and faith, continued to believe that the writing of this book (and the myriad babysitters) would, in fact end.

I thank you all.

Jené Stonesifer

*C*hildren are a gift from God; they are his reward.

Psalms 127:3

"*In* the interest of privacy and confidentiality,
all names have been changed."

TABLE OF CONTENTS

BREAKING THE RULES

First comes love,
Next comes marriage,
Then comes baby in the baby carriage

More than just a children's rhyme that some of us chanted as we skipped rope, the above passage represents the order in which nearly every woman believed, not so long ago, her life would unfold: a walk down the aisle, a champagne toast and a house backed with a swing set and a picket fence. In short, marriage *before* children.

But it doesn't always happen that way. It's time to recognize an alternative pattern: children outside of marriage. Historically viewed as an accidental variation, a stigma on the women concerned, this nontraditional family form is quickly becoming a viable alternative for women.

Perhaps you are on your way to joining the ranks. If so, you've got a lot of company. More than 1.2 million women gave birth outside of marriage in 1991 (the latest year for which statistics are available). That figure has more than doubled since 1980.

Critics of single parenting say the rapid increase mocks the significance of fathers and signals the breakdown of the family unit. Feminists see the option as a pure and simple right.

Regardless of your stance, it's empowering to realize that values, love, and commitment can remain just as strong in this new alternative family as in the old—as long as one is dedicated to that end and understands the unique issues involved.

If you are considering this path, you may find it comforting that social obstacles are disappearing. Television has helped bring single mothers into the mainstream with glamorous role models. The escalating success of women in the work force, meanwhile, coupled with the court's crackdown on delinquent fathers, has helped ease the financial burden of unmarried mothers. And single women who successfully give birth and raise children on their own from day one are scattered across the nation, inspiring all with whom they come in contact.

When Baby Makes Two salutes the decisions of mature women who have given birth after a surprise pregnancy—some without the emotional support of the child's father or even their own family members. It applauds women who possess enough belief in themselves as mothers and as caretakers to seek a child through adoption or artificial insemination. Nothing here, however, is intended to advocate irresponsible sexual relations or to undermine the importance of fathers.

As responsible single mothers, we must educate ourselves, acknowledging the special challenges of raising children in fatherless environments. We must make careful, well-thought-out decisions that will survive the test of time. We cannot afford to fail.

Meet the Moms

In the following chapters, we'll separate fact from fiction and explore the forces that compel some single women to begin parenthood alone. We'll do that largely by drawing on the firsthand experience of single mothers.

Mothers such as Rachel, a 38-year-old government employ-ee who went to her fiance´ to inform him of her unplanned preg-nancy. "Get an abortion," advised the man whose diamond she wore at the time.

And then there's Jennifer, who with the help of an anony-mous donor gave birth to a curly-haired girl whom she named Holly. A television producer who has always loved children, Jennifer used to joke that if she weren't married before a certain age, she would choose one of three ways of having a child: "I'm going to adopt, have artificial insemination or line up a hundred studs, blindfold myself and let them go at it." Unfortunately for the hundred studs, she chose artificial insemination—at age 45.

Two single mothers; two very different scenarios and psy-ches. For one mother, pregnancy was a crisis; for the other, it was a goal. They are examples of single mothers by chance and single mothers by choice.

Caught Off Guard

If, like Rachel, you are a single mother by chance, you decid-ed to keep and raise your child only after discovering you were pregnant. You may not have been overjoyed by the idea of moth-erhood at first. In fact, you may have been terrified.

In these pages, you'll hear from other women, between the ages of 23 and 43, who know that anguish—women whose emo-tions have vacillated between joyous anticipation of childbirth and heartbreak at a father's rejection.

Mothers will talk about how they felt after they were aban-doned by former lovers who knew of the pregnancy. They'll describe the rejection, fear and anger that stemmed from the lack of support. They'll tell us how they live with the startling reality of fathers who have never laid eyes on their own children. Imagine having to describe your child's biological father to him without having so much as a snapshot to share. Psychologists will offer you guidelines for answering questions about "Daddy" and let you know how to engage your child in conversations that quench his curiosity and boost his self-esteem.

We'll hear from women who have hammered out a healthy way to deal with negligent fathers on matters ranging from legal issues of child support, visitation and custody to unwritten codes of conduct in front of their children.

Going Ga-Ga

On the other hand, motherhood isn't always by accident, and the second part of the book focuses on single motherhood by choice—via artificial insemination, adoption or a relationship without strings.

Jennifer, the mother who joked about lining up one-night lovers, has yet to find a husband. Instead, she studied a sperm bank's catalog offering the genetic profiles of more than 200 men and eventually gave birth to a little girl, whom she hopes will one day help choose her own daddy.

Speaking of daddies, does Jennifer's daughter have one? That question raises a passionately controversial issue. Later, mothers and psychologists will talk about their stance regarding paternity, and a donor will discuss the accuracy (or lack thereof) with which he filled out the donor information sheet. He'll also share his feelings about being sought out by any children he may have fathered.

We'll look into the option of donors who are willing to have their identities released to their offspring down the road and explore the revolutionary possibility of seeking your own exclusive donor via a classified ad and a face-to-face meeting. Such an option can protect you from the anguish that comes of knowing your donor may have fathered numerous offspring and fearing your child may end up dating a relative. Of course, the section wouldn't be complete without addressing the delicate reality of talking to your child about his donor father and the gift of life he gave.

Like a support-group meeting, *When Baby Makes Two* introduces you to single mothers by choice, many of them in their late thirties and early forties, who yearn to be loved and depended upon by a youngster, as perhaps you do, too. The sight of a baby makes them drool. They want sippy cups and waterproof place mats, magnetic alphabet letters and high chairs cluttering their country kitchens; they would be delighted to have teddy bears underfoot and tops spinning around the baseboards of an extra bedroom.

They've satisfied their career goals and their materialistic needs; what they now yearn for is a child. Some are after the experience of giving birth; others want the opportunity to parent regardless of whether they themselves bear a child. All single mothers by choice long to immerse themselves in the issues and rituals of parenting—PTA meetings, car pools, the cloth-versus–disposable-diaper controversy.

But not all women confronted with the desire to parent are able to conceive and carry a child. And some women, from the very beginning, have an urge to parent but not to procreate. For them, adoption is another route toward motherhood.

The chapter on adoption touches on various types of adoptions, from international to private and special-needs adoptions, as well as the likelihood of a single mother's success in adopting in each of those ways. We'll also look at the costs, hear about the moments in which the mothers first eyed their children and the periods in which they learned to adjust to motherhood.

When Leigh brought her adopted daughter, Valerie, home to Sacramento, the four-year-old whirled through the house on a frantic search. After covering every inch, the youngster returned to her adoptive mother and blurted out, "There's no daddy in this home." She was disappointed, Leigh noted. But one year later, Valerie, who still has vivid and touching memories of her biological parents, is comfortable in her new home and emphatic in her new desire to become an adoptive mother when she grows up.

Common Ground

Nearly all single mothers realize the importance of male role models when a biological father is not available for a relationship with his child. Brothers, fathers and close male friends often fill the void, regularly spending time with the child. Other mothers make a point of socializing with a variety of people, including married couples with children, so that their child will see how a traditional family interacts.

Pro-family groups tout the importance of fathers to families, believing they help round out children socially. And too often, the possible lack of a resident father has swayed pregnant women into aborting their children or placing them up for adoption. I have noticed that an additional parent lightens a mother's stresses and allows for more laughter, giggles and gags.

But there is no need to agonize over the absence of a father. Research of traditional households by Karl Zinsmeister, a DeWitt Wallace Fellow at the American Enterprise Institute in Washington, D.C., provides a reality check that can be comforting to single mothers. Zinsmeister discovered that three-quarters of modern dads do not take regular responsibility for the daily care of their children. In fact, studies of children from kindergarten to tenth grade have found that daily father-child interplay averages only between 30 minutes and two and a half hours.

Where the Boys Are

Many pregnant single women worry that when they have their child, their potential supply of interested men will run dry. I have never found that to be the case. Successful, sensitive men who are willing to take on parental responsibilities are out there. In my estimation, a mother's ability to attract quality men remains equal to or greater than what it was when she was childless.

But during pregnancy until nearly a year after a child is born, many single mothers have little interest or energy left over for dating. As Rachel told me in her third month of pregnancy,

"Two of the men who stopped by my office today ended up flirting with me. I thought to myself, this is the last thing I'm interested in right now."

I've known some women who have gone on to marry and have more children. Others—because of their beautiful, gurgling, irresistible children—find themselves being approached by the opposite sex more often than ever before.

In spite of the turmoil, anguish and uncertainty that I experienced while seeking legal agreements and dealing with a disinterested father, I was able to meet a very special man just before my daughter turned five.

Of course, he wasn't there to catch Morgan when she passed through the birth canal, but he's there now to pick her up if she falls. And Morgan is thriving and blossoming from his attention. At 44 pounds, she's still light enough to enjoy the physical play that comes with a man's presence—being flopped over a set of wide shoulders and spun around in a crazy way, for instance. She's still young enough to enjoy climbing a gigantic dirt mountain with him in search of rocks and earthworms, and she's still impressionable enough to absorb his keen sense of humor and love of language. Although I had met several men before this one who were willing to be fathers, I hoped to meet my own needs also. And by virtue of example and commitment, I believe that this is one of the most precious and long-lasting gifts I will be able to give my daughter.

For Their Sake

Of utmost importance is the well-being of the child. All single mothers confront the challenges of time and money management, of being both disciplinarian and nurturer. Scads of books about single parenting address these issues, which apply to women who've lost their husbands through death or divorce , as well as those who've never married.

When Baby Makes Two explores the jolts and joys unique to single women who begin motherhood alone. It is meant to be a survival guide.

I wrote *When Baby Makes Two* for the sake of you single women and, more importantly, for your children. Ultimately, it is their comfort, health and happiness that matter the most and affect us all.

PART I

SINGLE MOTHERHOOD
by CHANCE

ONE

The Jolts and Joys of Single Motherhood by Chance

Reluctantly, I opened the brown paper bag and pulled out the pregnancy test kit. Having just shared my distress with a friend over the fact that I was experiencing the classic symptoms of pregnancy, I was fairly certain what the results would be. Sure enough, the liquid turned pink and confirmed my suspicions.

Being caught off guard by a pregnancy can be one of life's most terrifying and overwhelming experiences. Fears associated with the emotional and practical responsibility toward a child with a disinterested father roll through a single woman's mind. But it's possible to turn a surprise pregnancy and single motherhood into a rewarding, fulfilling reality. What it takes is a clear understanding of your emotions and your legal rights, and the working through of any related anguish; then the blessings will flow. Here we'll introduce you to the facts and feelings surrounding single motherhood by chance.

After allowing the reality of the positive pregnancy test results to set in, I, like most other single women distressed to find themselves pregnant, saw two alternatives flash before me. One was to abort the fetus, with a trip to the clinic and a check for several hundred dollars. My baby's father had told me that he was "not ready to be a father." But I was a believer in women's right to choose, and the idea of an abortion in this instance filled me with dread. I knew that was not the choice I wanted to live with.

That left me with the other alternative, to carry the baby to full term. A year out of college, I was living with my parents in Northern Virginia, trying to launch a local magazine that was breaking even after only two issues. In addition, I held two other part-time jobs, but I was still earning less than $20,000. I had no health insurance.

Yet my concerns about a future with an infant had less to do with making ends meet than with the possible reactions of those around me—my parents, my older brothers, friends of our family, the doctor for whom my mother worked, and one set of neighbors in particular—the two little girls who lived next to my parents and who looked up to me.

I *worried* about how the parents next door would explain my circumstances to their children. And after they had talked about "the situation," would the girls continue to enthusiastically scream "Hiiiiiii Jeneeeeee" from their driveway and across the gray rail fence dividing the houses whenever they saw me? Or would I now be looked upon as someone who was "bad"?

I was scared. But the greetings never stopped. My fears proved to be unfounded. The gestures of support sent our way through a strong internal network were too numerous to mention, but they included a preschool teacher who drove Morgan home once a week and a babysitter who treats her just like her very own grandchild. And when that family next door packed up for a move out West, they bequeathed a slew of toys to Morgan, including wooden puzzles, an Etch-a-Sketch and a bouncy hobbyhorse.

Coming Unglued

When 39-year-old Elizabeth learned that she was pregnant, she wasn't scared. Instead, she was elated—at first. Deeply in love with the father and financially stable in her own right, she was thrilled by the opportunity to be a parent. But when her boyfriend's opposition to the impending birth proved unshakable, she began to think the rewards of having a child might not be worth the emotional pain. Later, at a support-group meeting, she would recall her growing anxiety during the first few weeks of her pregnancy: "I felt at one point that if I had a gun I would have pointed it at my stomach and pulled the trigger."

Her numb despair lasted a couple of months. Now, just a few weeks away from giving birth, Elizabeth has accepted the father's lack of involvement and is throwing her energy into the things that she can offer her child. Decked out in designer maternity wear during a support-group meeting, she talked enthusiastically about the transformation of an extra room into a nursery and her search for a nanny.

The Road to Resentment

In the early days of pregnancy, the weight of your decision to have your child outside of marriage and the disappointment of discovering that the father-to-be is less than enthusiastic can be crushing. You didn't set out to get pregnant, and you may for a time feel overwhelmed by the magnitude of the responsibility and the complexity of some of the issues that lie ahead. I know I did. So much so, in fact, that at first I was unable to envision any of the positive repercussions motherhood would have on my life. It would have been impossible for me to believe that the experience would be the most valuable one of my life, one that has transformed me, making me more thoughtful, sensitive and giving.

The "glowing" pregnant woman and the "doting" father-to-be are common stereotypes even today. You don't hear much about pregnant women who are less than elated. When I was pregnant, however, I did not glow; my face was swollen and puffy from frequent bouts of crying as I tried to get used to the idea of single motherhood.

A knot sat in my stomach for weeks, and I worried that my heartache might hurt the fetus. Was I overreacting? Eventually, after running a notice in several newspapers saying that I was looking for women like myself, then talking with more than 100 of them, I found that my initial fears were not unusual. Many of the women went through periods of guilt and anger because of the father's reactions. But they didn't stay angry.

That's the difference between the victims and the survivors. Some remain fixed in their anguish and despair. Others grow from the jolt of pregnancy and find personal attributes that they didn't know existed. They fully experience the blessings of their pregnancy and motherhood.

The Survivors: You Can Be One

When you're not prepared for motherhood, an unexpected pregnancy can produce one of two reactions. It can turn you into a resentful, angry person, or it can strengthen and transform you into a more beautiful, resilient and more understanding one. Just because you weren't ready for motherhood doesn't mean you won't become a model parent for your child and find motherhood fulfilling. It may just take some work.

Devote yourself to that transition. You may find it helpful to learn about the anguish of women who cannot have children and who yearn to adopt; start by reading some of the other portions of this book, or turn to the personal notices of local newspapers to get a sense of other women's intense desire to parent. Knowledge of another woman's dream of motherhood can help cast a different light on your pregnancy.

If, six months after the birth of your child, you are still having problems progressing to a healthier mind-set, seek counseling. Support groups are another resource for venting emotions and measuring reality. If there isn't a support group for unmarried mothers in your area, consider starting one. You can do this by running an advertisement in your local newspaper. Meet in your living room. If that's not your style, use the ad to start a telephone network. Even a phone conversation with someone in your situation can help you see things differently and make better decisions. An ad to help you find someone like yourself might read: *"In Search of Unmarried Mothers. During a support-group meeting for unmarried mothers and pregnant women on June 15 at 7 P.M., in Northbrook, Illinois, we will discuss such things as legal issues and decisions related to paternity testing, child support, custody matters and emotions such as despair and anger that stem from feelings of abandonment. Call Jennifer, (503) 555-9000."*

Once you have a dozen or so women who want to gather regularly and learn more about the issues, you can pinpoint your needs and call in experts to speak to your group about the various challenges. For my group in Northern Virginia, we were able to bring in a family law attorney from the American Bar Association, a tax attorney who offered insight into wills and trusts, a domestic law judge who cleared up our misconceptions about visitation schedules and rulings on child custody and an expert on stress management. A woman who was born to an unmarried mother spoke to us about her childhood emotions upon realizing that most families have both a mom and a dad. The camaraderie coupled with the expert insight eased nearly all of our anxieties.

Single mothers by chance, armed with the will to succeed, are no less capable of being successful parents than women in a traditional family unit. Often, however, they are not mentally or economically prepared for motherhood.

Brooke, mother of 18-month-old Madeline, hadn't sought motherhood, and her shock communicated itself. "My family and friends couldn't even say, `That's great!'" she recalls. "Instead, they would look at me for a clue as to how they should react."

Ready or not, Brooke was forced to change from a free-spirited single woman into a responsible, nurturing single mother. Suddenly, she needed to be able to provide for a child. "I hadn't started looking at little undershirts or anything. It happened, and *then* I had to start planning," she says. In order to pay for diapers, day care and nursery equipment, most of us have to make drastic lifestyle changes.

Moving Toward Acceptance

Chances are you spend a great deal of time reflecting on the circumstances that led you to single motherhood. "How did this happen?" you may ask yourself again and again. "Is there anything I could do to make this relationship with my baby's father work? Do I want to make it work?" These are questions that a mother will need to resolve in her own mind. If you are like the majority of single mothers by chance, you feel a great deal of ambivalence about the pregnancy and about your relationship with your child's father.

Leah Keating, mother of a three-year-old son and assistant director of Mothers Alone, my support and educational group, noticed a pattern of emotions among the single mothers at our meetings. "They're usually ambivalent during the first three months of the pregnancy, then during the second trimester they begin to accept the pregnancy and see it as reality. There is more excitement, coupled with fear regarding the responsibility, during the third trimester."

How easily you accept your situation often depends on why you decided to parent alone. Perhaps you have opted to do so because you don't feel that you know your baby's father well enough to commit to him, yet you haven't completely ruled out marriage to him. Actress Sherilyn Fenn of *Twin Peaks* was in this situation when she became pregnant. "We're still getting to know each other," the actress told *People* magazine about her baby's father, a stagehand.

Or maybe the father made the choice. Even if you've had a long-term monogamous relationship, he may not have proposed marriage or offered any emotional support. Many of the fathers virtually deserted the mothers in our support group. "Get an abortion" was another common response. Such a statement can be downright shocking, and the pain can linger. "I question my judgment and how well I really know this man," stated Rachel, who was encouraged to abort by her fiancé.

The good news is that you can change your life by changing your thinking. Methods of doing so are included in chapter 3, which deals with accepting that whether a father is involved in his child's life isn't entirely up to you.

Fathers Have Legal Rights, Too

Even if it's difficult dealing with the biological father, his rights and responsibilities may make it necessary to do so. You may hope never to see him again, but he is not someone you can push away. Fathers have legal rights of visitation and may be very involved in their child's life, calling frequently to talk with him or dropping by every weekend to pick him up for outings or overnights.

Other fathers don't even acknowledge their children. You may only see the father of your child in the clinic for the blood tests to establish paternity or in the courtroom to solidify child support orders. He could change his mind down the road, and there is little you can do to prevent him from seeking, or avoiding, a relationship with his child.

Most mothers prefer to keep their dealings with the fathers of their children free of conflict. They see court battles as a last resort. I suggest you proceed in an amicable, informed and unantagonistic way. In addition to your own legal rights, you will need to familiarize yourself with those of fathers.

Many men are confused about the legal issues surrounding a child born outside of marriage. They are frightened and threatened and don't know how to handle the situation. They may employ tactics that they've been led to believe will somehow get them out of this situation. Try discussing things with your child's father first. If meetings together are uncomfortable or unproductive, outline your positions on legal issues in a letter to the child's father and suggest that he do the same.

Counseling, if your child's father is willing to make the commitment, or reference books on visitation and custody if he is prepared to devote time to reading them, can also help the two of you hammer out legal issues outside of the courtroom. If you are unable to reach an agreement, however, you may need to take certain issues before a judge.

Grace, 25, still harbors some anger because her daughter's father walked away during her pregnancy but is now back in their lives and entitled to keep his nine-month-old daughter, Madison, for four days a month. "I'm home with her when she has a temperature of 103. *He* gets the benefit of the good part of

Madison—taking her to his office, showing her off, having fun with her."

Yet Grace complies and is flexible with Bob's requests to see Madison. He has interacted with her since she was born, and Grace knows that the courts would view his requests as reasonable. "The hardest thing to do is separate how I feel about him and what is best for Madison," notes Grace. It's taken "a lot of trial and error" to work out arrangements. "We tolerate each other. And I remind myself frequently that what's best for Madison is that she know her mom *and* her dad."

Anna, whose former boyfriend vowed that he would fight to maximize visitation if she took him to court for child support, sees it this way: "There's an added stress level, an anxiety and an anger that surface when consulting with a lawyer or arguing over an issue, and I often wonder, why should my kids be subjected to this crap?

"It's easy to get so tied up in the problems of being a single mom that you lose the joy that goes with it. I have to constantly remind myself not to let that happen."

What He Doesn't See Can't Hurt Him: Uninvolved Fathers

Many biological fathers never even meet their children. And if you're like most mothers, you may buy into the notion that if your child's father would only see his son or daughter, he would beovertaken by such beauty and charm and instantly devote himself to parenting responsibilities. Such rejection can be devastating. I've seen many a mother torment herself because her child's father was just not interested in a relationship with his child.

Brooke's former lover, a married man, has seen his 18-month-old just once. "And even then, he wouldn't hold her," she lamented. He just happened to see the strawberry-blond infant when he stopped by Brooke's house to drop off some legal paperwork. Brooke had extended an open visitation offer to her daughter's father, an attorney, but he made it clear to her that he was not in a position to become emotionally involved with his daughter. "He doesn't ask about Madeline and he's never visited her formally. He's never said, `I'd like to take Madeline to the zoo.' He's not interested in being her dad."

Brooke understands the rationale behind her married man's inability to commit emotionally to their daughter. But for mothers dealing with single fathers who don't have such a plausible excuse, the acceptance of this reality can be even tougher. "It's incredibly painful," notes Carmen, whose three-year-old son, Jason, has never caught a glimpse of his father, much less been tossed up in the air by him. "He knows other people have daddies and he doesn't," concludes Carmen. "One night, I was giving Jason a bath and he just blurted, out of the blue, `Daddy gone,' and I said, `Yes, Daddy's in California.'"

Psychologists and family courts generally support the relationship between a father and his child. But paternal love is not something that can be forced, although some women have been known to try. In fact, 13 years ago, in California, a single mother attempted to get a court order to require that the father regularly visit his child. She lost the case; what she saw as the right of her child to a nurturing paternal relationship, the court saw as involuntary servitude.

With an angry or just uncooperative biological father may come legal tussles. You might be the one to initiate legal action, if you are in need of child support and the father is not willing to provide it without a court order. Disgruntled fathers do occasionally retaliate by pushing for partial custody and visitation rights.

Here Comes the Sun

Getting beyond your resentment and anger at an uninvolved or uncooperative father takes work. When I was pregnant, the worst-case scenarios flowing through my mind with regard to Morgan's father had to do with monetary issues and where our daughter would spend holidays. It never occurred to me that he would shun his child and not see her until she was four years old.

If you are like most mothers, you hope for a healthy relationship between your child and his father. If that does not come to fruition, you may need to mourn the absence of your child's father's love. It's perfectly natural. But keep moving forward. If you've handled things properly, you may be able to derive peace from knowing that you've behaved honorably. Try to make decisions and take steps that will survive the test of time.

Carmen, who has not seen her lover since the day she told him she was pregnant, consoles herself with the knowledge that she has done all that she can logically do to encourage a relationship. "I always try to remember that what's important is what's right for Jason." In offering Jason's father a relationship, she says, "I have done all that I can do. I feel like I've been fair and reasonable. I feel comfortable with the way I've handled things."

Another way to move along is to focus on what you can offer your child. Try listing those assets of yours that will enrich your child's life. Your list may range from such concrete things as a safety-approved car seat and a bedroom to such forms of emotional support as tenderness and sensitivity. You can also include character traits that you would like to encourage and shape through example, such as charm, drive and financial know-how.

As your baby grows, the rewards you experience will be more explicit, like the unexpected kiss and hug Carmen received as she read the newspaper one Sunday. "It's an affirmation that we're a family," she concluded, "and all that matters is that we love each other."

Bouncing Back: The Road to Self-Empowerment

Even if you've been thrust into single parenting, you will experience incomparable joy when you first lay eyes on the precious infant you've created and hold a bundle that will forever change the way you see the world. Ultimately, motherhood can bring about a tremendous amount of personal growth and satisfaction.

Moving from a me-first, egotistical phase of life to one in which a child's needs take priority can be especially difficult for the mother who was not eager to make such a transition. It is particularly frustrating when you are virtually the only one to meet those needs. Success very often involves a change in thinking, good coping skills and a hefty dose of creativity.

In her early twenties, Grace would blow up and walk away in a huff when things didn't go her way. She attributes the deepening of her tolerance to the birth of her baby girl. "You learn to take a deep breath, come back and start over again. I'm not saying I'm perfect, but I have some patience now, where before I had none."

The birth of a child gives a parent a tangible reason to succeed and excel. Most mothers set their sights higher than they did before their children were born. Before my daughter was conceived, I wasn't earning a substantial living, but I didn't really mind. I didn't have a game plan.

When it became clear during my pregnancy that I would be the primary provider for my child, I was forced to sit down and draw one up. Health benefits, savings plans, investments, real-estate down payments and a career strategy suddenly occupied my thinking. Motherhood was a sink-or-swim proposition for me, but one for which I will be forever grateful. Being responsible for my daughter has stepped up my level of responsibility for myself.

The dent in their social life is often one of the biggest changes faced by single mothers by chance. But few seem to mind. "What's that?" joked one single mother when the subject of dating came up. Her social contact with the other sex now consists mainly of a weekly Sunday dinner she hosts for a former beau who fulfills a godfatherly role for her four-year-old daughter.

Brooke believes that dating will become easier now that her daughter is nearing age 2. "It has not been a priority at all," she confided. "If I had a date, it would include Madeline. It might be to the zoo or to the pet-a-pet farm."

Other single mothers make a point of dating and social-izing. "I go out at least twice a week," says Danielle, a vibrant woman who pays her child-care provider overtime in order to enjoy regular escapes. "I usually go to happy hour once a week and get home in time to see my son before he's put down to bed; other times, I'll head out after I've put him down to sleep."

Dates do have a way of taking on a very different tone when you are a single mother. It's no longer enough that a man be handsome, successful and fun-loving. You are shopping for two now. And other traits, such as dependability, a capacity for nurturing and an interest in family life have a way of rising to the top of the heap of priorities.

A child is an invaluable asset when you're out in the dat-ing world. Your child is your screen. Although I have never personally met a man who shuddered when I mentioned that I had a child, I remember wishing a few of them had turned on their heel and walked out of sight at the news. But if I did meet one with these feelings, I would consider myself fortunate to have discovered so quickly that he was not interested in a com-mitted relationship to a family.

Watching a man you are serious about interact with your child can tell you volumes about the type of person he is. My growing interest in one man was was clenched when I saw him patiently jog across a horse track with Morgan on his back so that she could pet a Thoroughbred for the nth time. I grew more attracted while listening to him read Morgan a bedtime story. His ad-libbing of a little girl's cat-sitting adventure had both Morgan and me nearly wetting our pants with laughter.

Parenting requires a partnership, yet couples who are courting without children never have the opportunity to put those nuturing skills to the test. I remember my dates before my daughter was born. I assumed that all men, certainly the ones I dated, would be good with children. But I feel certain now that many married women would have chosen their husbands differently had they actually been able to glimpse their parenting skills in action.

The Joy Is in the Child

As Lisa, a graduate nursing student and the mother of a three-year-old, sees it, "Justin was the catalyst that started my real adult life. I don't know where I would be today without him." Most of us share that wonder.

The joy of raising a child—how can I describe it? It's the fun of witnessing the first blown dandelion, the first footprint in the snow; it's the pleasure of applauding my daughter's patio performance as I hum the familiar *Nutcracker* tunes. Moments like those reinforce my satisfaction with the decision to defy social convention and family concern, to have and raise Morgan despite an absentee father and my own uncertain circumstances. I made the right choice; of that I am sure.

That is not to say that there are not discouraging times. But whenever I feel frustrated with my lot, anxious about finances, depressed at outside opportunities missed, I think of my favorite Morgan tale of late: It was bedtime and we were saying good night. I was explaining the reason for the saying "Sweet dreams." Morgan had never talked to me about any of her dreams, and I had wondered if she remembered any of them or realized what they were. "Sometimes dreams are funny. Other times they're exciting, sad or even scary," I explained. "So `Sweet dreams' is a wish for nice, happy ones."

From the bed came the already drowsy voice as I turned out the light. "I hope I'll dream *you*," said Morgan.

Who could ask for more?

CHAPTER 2

When the Results Are Positive

and Daddy Isn't

Few fathers embrace the mother warmly or hand out cigars when hit with the news of an unforeseen pregnancy. More often, the reaction is passive support, the silent treatment or desertion. Many men express their preference for a quick and easy end to the crisis with a three-word response: "Get an abortion."

The father's reaction to the pregnancy usually has a lot to do with his level of devotion to the mother. Men find the idea of fathering a child with a woman they are not in love with disturbing.

Of course, there are unmarried fathers who are thrilled at the news of an impending offspring. Unexpected pregnancies have motivated many couples to rush joyfully down the aisle or into a courthouse. Shotgun weddings, on the other hand, are rare nowadays. If the father-to-be isn't truly enthusiastic about a union, it isn't likely to happen.

And in spite of their smiles for the press and public show of devotion to one another, we don't know how high-profile unmarried couples—Jerry Hall and Mick Jagger; Marla Maples and Donald Trump before they tied the knot—reacted to the news that they were to become parents.

The entire nation witnessed actor William Hurt being dragged into court by his thumbs by former New York City ballerina Sandra Jennings on a paternity matter after living with her for three years. Hurt pays $65,000 annually in child support for his son, Alexander, according to a *Washington Post* report in 1990. The highly publicized video clips of his angry outbursts in court entertained many who were watching evening tabloid-news programs on television.

Less-than-joyful reactions from dads can have an emotional effect on the women bearing their children. Here, we'll explore the range of feelings of mothers dealing with men who resent their decision to keep their babies. You will hear from mothers whose turmoil may mirror your own. And you will learn a strategy for transforming extreme emotions into a more healthy mental state.

Informing the Father

You probably have some idea as to how your child's father will react when you deliver the news of your pregnancy. Perhaps you envision him reassuring you of his support and emotional backing regardless of your decision. But be prepared to see a side of the father that you never knew existed. This is the ultimate test.

Use discretion and good taste when you inform him about your pregnancy. One mother I knew sent the father a congratulations-on-your-new-baby card that showed a chimpanzee holding a rattle, which went over like a lead balloon. Whether to share the news in person, on the telephone or in a letter is a very personal decision. But above all, try to be sensitive to the nature of the news and the way it will change your lives forever.

Some women, fearing retaliation or the constant presence and interference of a man they don't care for, decide never to inform the father of their pregnancy. Unless the father is somehow dangerous, I can only see such deception working against you. Your child may grow up believing that if only his father had known about him, his life would have been perfect. Don't make that mistake; it may only give your child's father an excuse to avoid a relationship with his child. Some fathers justify never meeting their children by denying that they were ever told about them.

It is a good idea to inform the father about the birth of a child in writing, as well as in conversation. That way, he will be held accountable for his actions. It is essential that you allow him to choose whether to participate in his child's life by letting him know about his offspring.

Some fathers confront the news of a surprise pregnancy with hostility. Usually, this is due to a man's inability to have any control over the situation and the environment. Such loss of control is frightening to men.

For example, soon after sharing the news of her pregnancy with her companion of about six months, Valerie received a hand-delivered Valentine's Day surprise. Upon answering a knock at the door, the 32-year-old communications specialist, then just a few weeks pregnant, received not a bouquet of red roses or a box of bonbons but a letter from the lawyer representing her son's father, demanding that she have an abortion.

Another young mother-to-be, Lisa, was left standing in a hospital parking lot in a cloud of exhaust after telling the father, a surgeon, about her pregnancy and her desire to keep the baby. "I have no interest in you; I have no interest in this child," he told the 23-year-old hospital clerk before speeding away in his red Porsche.

Within weeks of sharing the news of her pregnancy with her former lover, Laura discovered her tires slashed as she was about to drive home from work.

Even Cindy's move across country to escape the hostility of her daughter's father didn't reduce his anger toward her. Soon after the move, she received a two-page letter from his best friend, attacking her and her decision to keep and raise the child. "It's too bad you can't have a child with a man who wants one," the friend stated. "It's too bad you have no friends, don't feel better about yourself." In so many words, the letter attributed her decision to have the baby to a personal vendetta against the father. "I'm sure my daughter's father put him up to it," concludes Cindy.

Not all reactions from the fathers I've heard of were quite so dramatic. But a recurring factor in these women's stories was the father's skepticism about the pregnancy claim. Many women were asked to take a pregnancy test in the father's presence.

A more neutral reaction came from Danielle's live-in lover upon learning the truth behind his girlfriend's recent nausea. At first, he was dead silent. Then the 45-year-old father of two grown children "proceeded to pour himself the biggest glass of Scotch I've ever seen," recalls Danielle.

The unanticipated pregnancy invokes these reactions for a number of reasons. Some men believe that they were trapped, handpicked because of their good looks or position in life. They choose to see the pregnancy as an attempt to get them to the altar or as a trick to keep them forever chained.

A few actually imagine that the mother of their child is seeking child-support money that she can spend on luxuries for herself. Thinking the worst of a mother and denouncing her as crazy reduces their sense of responsibility toward the child. Echoing the "It's not my fault" defense of Lorena Bobbitt, the Menendez brothers and Tonya Harding, they choose to be victims. Some see the pregnancy purely as a financial drain or a crimp in their social life. Yet in spite of such rocky starts, some of these same fathers do become very devoted to their children.

There are times, of course, when it's the father who is overjoyed by the pregnancy, and the mother who is putting distance between them. Either way, each party's emotions can swing wildly as the pregnancy progresses and stances are made clear, at times through legal actions.

Dealing With the Father's Reaction

Once you've told your baby's father about the news, you may have a pretty good idea of whether he is able to support you in this matter. For your own sanity, I urge you to lower your expectations with regard to your baby's father and prepare to take some personal attacks and criticism. But don't dwell on them or take spiteful comments personally.

Instead, concentrate on yourself and your importance to your baby. Realize that the only person that you and your child can fully rely on is you. If your baby's father does lend emotional and/or financial support, perhaps after being forced to by the legal system, you'll have more than you counted on.

Give your baby's father time to digest the news of your pregnancy. And while he's doing that, throw your energy into positive extracurricular activities, such as an exercise class for women who are expecting, a sewing class to make a baby comforter or a short course on homemade baby foods. And leaf through books on time and money management.

Nancy, a graduate student, was invited by her lover to celebrate the impending birth of their child over lunch. But soon after she conveyed that she no longer wanted an intimate relationship with him, she found herself the focus of a scandalous rumor related to her lack of sexual discretion, which she believes he started. "But I let it go," says Nancy, whose one-year-old, Jennifer Lynn, sees her father about twice a month. Nancy chose to ignore the rumor and has since virtually forgotten about it. "Things are fine now."

Nancy's decision not to dwell on the pain and embarrassment the rumor caused is a good example of dealing effectively with an uncooperative father. Such dealings can take a lot of work and tolerance, but it's important that you surmount this challenge and begin to heal. Methods for coping with feelings of rejection and abandonment are addressed later in this chapter.

It is almost impossible for anyone who has not experienced it firsthand to imagine the anguish felt by the unmarried mother as she decides to raise her baby alone. A society that by now is fully aware of the grief associated with infertility, abortion and the placement of babies for adoption has yet to tune in to the unmarried mother's emotional distress.

The inner turmoil that begins when the father expresses his displeasure is sharpest for younger women—women between the ages of 18 and 25. For them, pregnancy is apt to be not just a surprise but a mind-numbing shock.

These women are usually either students or have only recently joined the work force. They may be living on scholarships, parental donations or salaries barely above the minimum wage. Their home may be a dormitory, a shared town house or an efficiency apartment. Keeping the child may mean corporate or low-budget day care rather than a nanny; it will likely mean a crib in the corner of the room rather than in a nursery with designer linens and wallpaper.

For these young women, motherhood may well mean a return to the home they just left. Perhaps they will have to work an extra job, give up a planned career, or at the very least, enlist the help of a parent for such things as shuffling a child to or from day care.

Unlike more mature mothers-to-be, young women generally have immediate concrete expectations of the father, his relationship to them and, more important, to the child. Rather than mere disappointment, they may feel the anger and hurt of perceived betrayal. One young woman, although "quietly pleased," when she learned of her pregnancy, went on to agonize over the father's initial reluctance to be involved in his son's life other than to support him financially. "Here is this person, the only other person who can ever love my child the way I can—and he doesn't want him," cried Lisa.

When Lisa's former lover, a respected surgeon, finally met his son, the child was nearing his second birthday. Lisa wept with joy at the sight and later recalled in a whisper, "It was beautiful and very satisfying. I knew Justin was incredible, and I could sense that Don felt it too. It was an affirmation that our son was a precious and wonderful thing." Two years later, Justin has a stable relationship with his father and his stepmother. Lisa is stronger emotionally because she knows that her son's other parents are behind her and all of her related decisions. "I am so happy for my son, because now he has his father's love. I am at peace now."

Rebecca's live-in relationship with her daughter's father ended with the announcement of her pregnancy. His vicious final comments during a long-distance telephone conversation—"What? Are you *crazy*? I don't *love* you; I'm not going to *marry* you"—were enough to make the 23-year-old mother-to-be consider putting her child up for adoption.

"Without the emotional or financial support of my baby's father, I saw it being a huge struggle for the first year and a half," says Rebecca, who needed that time to finish earning her nursing degree at Georgetown University. "I figured it would cost me at least $160 a week in child care. And I kept thinking about the hardship of not being able to share the baby with anyone. He [the baby's father] didn't ask me how I was doing or how I felt, so I could just imagine taking care of the baby and not having anyone to turn to, and not having anyone to tell that the baby smiled today."

A former Club Med employee who loves to travel, Rebecca had always had trouble staying in one place. She had made a conscious effort to rid her life of material possessions that might inhibit her get-up-and-go.

But part of her held back from the notion of giving up her child. "I had the feeling that it was *my* son or daughter, and it was exciting to think that someone might look like me or have my talent, characteristics or abilities," Rebecca declares. "I've read that adopted children have a lower self-esteem, a feeling of rootlessness. They wonder why they were given up. I didn't want to wonder if my child would find me someday and I would feel like I had to apologize and say, 'I didn't want to give you up.'"

Fortunately, Rebecca didn't have to make such a choice. Two months after the phone conversation that ended the amorous relationship, her baby's father proposed. A whirlwind wedding and handmade baby announcements from the parents of Mary Elizabeth, eight pounds, three ounces, followed.

When the dust has settled, unmarried mothers-to-be display a pattern of emotions that varies slightly depending on the father's reaction to the pregnancy.

If his response is extremely negative, the cycle may begin with a mother's feelings of shame and confusion. You may feel somewhat embarrassed that you had intimate relations with and so misjudged a man who could not support you in this matter. "Even if he asked me to marry him right now, I don't think I could," confided Maria about her former fiancé, based upon his wish for her to abort. "I keep asking myself, how well did I really know this individual?"

When confronted with an angry father, most women feel frightened. "He threatened to take the baby away from me," a terrified Melissa told other single mothers during a support-group meeting. Her fear stemmed from the father's vindictive statements and the legal actions he claimed were available to him. Other women are terrified by the responsibilities of giving birth to a child.

"Imagine being scared to death," says Joe Soll, a clinical social worker and director of New York City's Council for Equal Rights in Adoption, a governmental advocacy organization on adoption rights. "They want their baby, they're afraid of their family, they're afraid people are going to call them bad names, and the father questions paternity and doesn't want anything to do with them." Women often say to Soll, "I can't think straight," and he tells them, somewhat reassuringly, "It's no wonder."

Another person familiar with the anguish of single pregnant women is Dr. Helen A. Mendes. Mendes, who runs a counseling service for single parents in Los Angeles, sees single mothers most often when their relationship with the father is deteriorating and when they are experiencing a great deal of ambivalence. On one hand, an unwed mother "wants to salvage the relationship with the father"; on the other hand, "she wants to get out."

The reason for the ambivalence is quite simple. "Most people know or believe that children should have two parents. When it looks like the father is not going to be involved, they begin to feel as if their child will be cheated," explains Mendes, who often helps mothers decide whether to struggle to hang on to the relationship with the father or to move forward and look for someone else who can meet some of the child's needs.

It is perfectly natural to experience guilt, confusion and anger for a while. Perhaps in the heat of the moment you didn't use birth control. Many mothers, even those who had no desire to get pregnant, feel a twinge of guilt for having not used birth control. In so many cases, however, the father did not use a condom. It takes two, and the guilt, if any, in this situation should be shared. Another source of guilt has to do with the mother's desire to provide a traditional family unit for her child when it may not be feasible for her to do so.

Counseling helped Carmen, 32, move beyond her feelings of guilt and realize that while she did have to accept responsibility for herself and for her actions, she did not have to accept it for Jeremy, her son's father. "I didn't have to accept responsibility for ruining Jeremy's life, damaging his career, our relationship and all of the other things he blamed me for."

Moving On: Freeing Yourself From Fear

Feelings of anger, which usually follow fear and guilt, may surface when a mother becomes informed about her child's rights and aware of which of the father's statements she should take seriously and which she can afford to ignore. Knowledge is the best medicine. It can reassure the single mother; it can empower her.

After an initial consultation with a lawyer or a meeting with a support group, single mothers often experience a dramatic increase in confidence. This is because during these sessions, factors that influence child support, custody and visitation are made clear.

I'll never forget how much better I felt after learning from a family-law attorney that the threats of my daughter's father—to declare bankruptcy so I wouldn't receive child support, and to get so much visitation time that I wouldn't ever see my daughter or even recognize her—didn't hold water.

Fears that stem from the comments of your child's father may dissolve once you have a basic knowledge of family law in your jurisdiction. Schedule a consultation with a family-law attorney or attend a support-group meeting for single mothers as soon as possible. Given the facts, you'll find it much easier to proceed confidently and wisely.

Putting Your Anger to Work

When angry, mothers have been known to turn the memory of searing comments and feelings of desertion into an all-out pursuit of their child's legal rights, beginning with child support. The family court has a reputation as an emotional battlefield. The good thing about this type of action is that it's constructive. Keep your anger channeled into actions that are beneficial for both you and your child.

"Being angry and resentful is very self-serving but not at all rewarding," concludes Carmen. "It takes a lot of work." And for the most part, it is the parent who is angry who suffers the most. In addition to leaving you physically and emotionally drained, anger can take away from your natural beauty.

But recent studies of the emotion have shown that it is possible to transform anger into energy. Instead of attempting to suppress anger and harness it, try using the energy to do something productive, such as exercise. Take a long walk, wash your car or organize your closets. These kinds of tasks, unlike blowing up at a retail clerk or putting your car's pedal to the metal, will give you an added sense of accomplishment.

Next, make a plan to handle the anger-provoking person or situation in the future. Many of us have received letters from the fathers of our children that have thrown us into a rage. A father's unfulfilled promises to our children are another frequent source of anger.

Instead of fretting over letters, conversations or broken promises, resolve to bring up any legal concerns with a lawyer the next day or put your ire to work at the gym. Isn't a workout that leaves your biceps and thighs looking perfectly sculpted in a bathing suit much more rewarding? Keep the anger working for you and your child rather than against you.

Another way to handle anger effectively is to transform it into more healthy feelings. When a single mother is feeling either angry or horrified about the circumstances of her pregnancy, Albert Ellis, president of the Institute for Rational-Emotive Therapy in New York, helps her change her feelings, often over a period of just a few weeks, into healthier emotions such as sorrow, disappointment or regret.

First, Ellis, a psychologist who has been counseling single mothers for 50 years, explains to a mother that she will need to accept reality and that "if she doesn't, she will feel depressed and horrified, and that won't do her or her child any good."

One of the techniques he recommends for coping with anger is the Serenity Prayer by philosopher Reinhold Niebuhr:

"God, give us the grace to accept with serenity the things that cannot be changed, courage to change the things which should be changed, and the wisdom to distinguish the one from the other."

If it is an uninvolved father whom the single mother is upset about, Ellis reassures her that it is all right to regret that her child doesn't have a father who takes an interest in them. "It's also unfortunate that you don't have a million dollars," he adds in the same breath.

The point Ellis makes is that "you don't need to upset the child about this." The child has a choice as to whether he will be upset about this, and "he can be taught not to be upset about this," says Ellis. "He needs to understand that the two of you can still lead a happy existence."

Finally, after helping the single mother change her way of thinking and feeling, Ellis works on modifying her behavior. For instance, if depression or anger is causing her to neglect her child in some way or keeping her in the house, afraid to date again, Ellis pushes her to perform certain tasks, such as setting dental appointments for her child or attending social events, that she finds uncomfortable. "I get her to realize that when things don't work out, it's too bad—it's not *awful* or *terrible*—and when they do, it's good."

Leaving Rejection Behind

Much of your emotional trauma may be due to the fact that you were in love with the baby's father. You may be hurting first and foremost for yourself, because of the ending of a once-promising relationship. If that's the case, you will need to work through your heartache.

Mendes likes to focus on goals and reality with her patients. She begins by asking them what they want. Some want the love of the child's father. At the very least, most of them would like their child to have the father's love. After exploring the possibilities of such desires—considering, for instance, whether your child's father is married or has expressed any interest at all in his child—you may want to take steps that lead you closer to your goal, or you may decide that such a desire isn't an option and it's best to accept reality.

How to get over the rejection of a lover was one of the questions most frequently asked of counselors, according to a 1990 article that included advice from Ellis and was published in *Cosmopolitan.*

"Your obsession results from your defining this one person—out of five billion people on earth—as not just desirable but *necessary,* which simply isn't true," Ellis pointed out. "No matter how special and wonderful you think this man is, there are many others with whom you'd be as happy—or happier."

It can be extremely difficult and painful to be linked permanently through a child to a man whom you may love and who may not love you. But it's important to realize that a mother experiencing heartache is not able to offer her child as much as someone who is emotionally stable. A combination of time and changes in your actions and thinking will help you move on.

For me, the hardest thing to overcome was the lost relationship between my daughter and her father. It was a natural feeling for me to want my daughter's father to take a sincere and devoted interest in her, and I could not accept the reality overnight.

Over time, I was able to find peace in accepting the reality of the lost relationship. I learned that a mother may have to settle for peace, rather than whatever situation she desires. Instead of being consumed with sadness over the rejection of my child or anger at her being cheated, I contented myself with extending the offer of a relationship to my daughter's father. The choice not to be involved was his, and he knows how to find us. I doubt that we will ever see my daughter's father at one of her ballet recitals or school concerts, but by making long-term decisions based on my daughter's well-being rather than my pride, I found peace.

A Single-Parenting Plan

The truth is, the actions of your child's father are beyond your control. Therefore, one way to empower yourself is to develop a single-parenting plan, a plan that doesn't involve him. Check libraries and bookstores for handbooks that explore the practical aspects of single parenting, from time management to dating and disciplining your child.

Reading such materials and finding answers to the questions that come up along your personal journey to motherhood—such as where you will give birth, how much it will cost, how much time you can take off from work and how to screen child-care establishments—can help propel you out of your woes.

Mendes explores the realities of single parenting with each client. "I get her to think about who will be there for her if she gets sick or wants to take a vacation, whether she has enough money for a housekeeper, and whether she has people she can kick back with and be a person with or whether she will build her life around the child."

Feeling Good About the Family

The light at the end of the tunnel *will* come, rest assured. Perhaps it will take the form of a better adjustment to your life circumstances, a change of heart on the father's part or legal resolution to the problems between you, making it easier to dismiss past wrongs.

In spite of an initial negative reaction, some fathers do come around. Others send money voluntarily or offer to baby-sit. The man in the red Porsche mentioned earlier in this chapter, who roared off in a fury, leaving the mother of his child standing in a cloud of exhaust, has always been forthcoming with financial support. He even informed Lisa about the military hospital and commissary privileges that she could take advantage of with their son because of his military service. He has extended visits with his son at least twice a year.

For Rebecca, the woman who was initially deserted by the man who later became her husband, the episode turned out to have a fairy-tale ending. She was in love with her baby's father. Marriage to your child's father may not be what you consider a fairy-tale ending, or his hand may not be offered. You can still go on to lead a joyful and enriching life with your child.

Mothers of children with disinterested fathers often feel a lingering sense of sadness and rejection on behalf of the child if the father continues to shun his son or daughter. Consultations with family professionals and child psychiatrists can ease a mother's concern over a child's possible sense of rejection, but I don't believe the longing ever leaves a conscientious mother's mind altogether.

One single mother who yearned for the involvement of her son's father in his life got upset just by seeing another father interact with his child on a playground, pushing him on a swing. Another mother had similar feelings when her son was nearly two. "I still get jealous when I see children my son's age with fathers who are actively involved in their lives," admits Carmen, whose son, Jason, has never met his father. She herself has not seen the man since she announced that she was pregnant. "But it's getting easier. And as painful as it is, being honest is the only thing that helps me move forward."

Regardless of a father's initial reaction or presence, you may still be able to facilitate a healthy working relationship between him and his child. Be patient, keep your emotions under control and strive to make decisions that you can reflect back on with pride. Often, giving space and time to the father can be your most valuable gifts during the early months of the pregnancy.

THREE

Will Your Child's Biological

Father Be "Daddy"?

Remember *Make Room for Daddy*, the old TV sitcom? Its title implies a world of vexing issues for any woman who is raising a child on her own. Should she make room for the biological father in her child's life, or for that matter, in her life? What will be the effect on them if she does? How should she go about it? And what if he's of a different mind?

Most mothers, of course, do hope that the father of their child will take an interest in his offspring. There are a few, however, who will go to great lengths to discourage such involvement, sometimes in order to protect their children or themselves from further emotional scarring.

To involve the father or not—that may be the most passionate question for mothers in single-parent households. As some of the following examples make clear, however, the real problem may be how to accept the reality that Daddy's involvement is not entirely up to her. The ultimate challenge may be to address the extent of his presence in a way that will not scar the child.

Wanting and Not Wanting the Father Involved

The Fact that her two-year-old son has never seen his father conjures up an array of emotions for Carmen. "I probably think about it every day," she says. "My biggest desire is that my son's father will see Jason and try to develop a relationship with him *immediately*, so that Jason will remember always being involved with him.

"My greatest fear," she continues, "is that my son's father will choose never to see him and that someone will walk up to him and say, `Your Dad must be proud of you,' and Jason will have to say, `I've never met my father.'"

"It's something I lie awake at night worrying about," admits Danielle, 26, two months before she was about to give birth. "I worry that if I have a boy, he won't have a male role model."

Charlene's son sees his father quite regularly. Through an informal arrangement, baby Brandon spends two weekends a month with Kurt, who also acted as Charlene's birthing coach. Kurt visits Brandon at Charlene's home or takes his son back for a weekend at his own home, nearly four hours away. But for Charlene, the arrangement is a mixed blessing.

"It's a catch-22," she admits, explaining that she still feels anger about the past each time she sees Kurt. "We have a communication problem, and there are times when he should call me [and ask for advice] with regard to our son, and he doesn't." On two occasions, Brandon has returned home ill after visits with his father—once with pneumonia and another time with diarrhea. Charlene soon learned that her one-year-old son's diarrhea was caused by a slice of pizza topped with "the works."

Even Carmen, who craves the involvement of her son's biological father, is afraid of the feelings that it might stir up in her. "Jeremy as `Daddy' implies a level of involvement that makes me uncomfortable right now. I wonder, how will Jeremy's life compare to mine? If he's going to be in my face as Jason's Dad, I don't want to be envying his lifestyle or feeling resentful. I want to be moving ahead with my own life."

Even with regular, healthy interaction between a father and his child, the nature of the relationship between parents often changes, and that can cause discontent. "We're like a married couple without the sex," complains Elaine, a 39-year-old computer programmer and the mother of one-year-old Jamie. "We go out to dinner every Sunday, take day trips together and visit the grandparents as a family." But while enjoying the family-like atmosphere, Elaine misses the sexual intimacy.

No decision or pattern with regard to these relationships is permanent. A father who has expressed virtually no interest in a child may change his outlook after several years; one who has grasped the child's heart may not make time for him when a new love interest appears.

It's important to remember that a father's stance toward a child, whatever that may be, may change at any point in the child's life. Just as you've finally accepted the situation, he may change his tune. Flexibility is essential.

It took the father of Lisa's son nearly 18 months to express a desire to see his child. Lisa, a nursing student at Marymount University in Arlington, longed for this day, but when she received a letter from Don signaling his interest, she realized that she was not only glad but nervous. "I was hoping, for Justin's sake, that Don would take an interest in him, but then I was afraid that he would take him [away from me]," says Lisa. "I was frightened because I knew that as a surgeon he had all the resources, including money to spend freely on lawyers. I was living with my family and knew that any extraordinary legal costs would have to be covered by my father."

Another issue troubled Lisa. "I had always thought of my son as mine, and I knew that now I would have to share him."

Today, Don, who is married, boards a plane to visit his son or has the toddler and his mother flown to his home about three times a year. He also calls every Saturday and sends holiday care packages regularly, from coloring books to Easter baskets and expensive motorized riding toys.

Now Lisa says she wishes that her son's father and his wife lived closer. Lisa, who will marry next spring, feels certain she could share Justin with his other two parents. At this point, "it's such a big emotional thing, since their visits are few. It's hard to get back down to earth after them."

My daughter's father, Steve, met his child for the first time shortly after her fourth birthday. When she was 18 months old, he had declared, "I just don't think I would be a very good father figure."

A few mothers don't want to tell the fathers about their children. Some even move across the country in an effort to prevent a relationship from developing between them. More common is the mother who forgoes her child's right to support, fearing the father will expect visitation privileges in return.

Some men do pursue short-term visitation with their child as a means of retaliating against the mother and in the hope of getting child support reduced. But it's possible to prepare a child for a father who may not be consistent in his visits by presenting him as someone who is interested in him but not necessarily a regular fixture in his life. For your child's sake, don't make the mistake of alluding to a long-term relationship with his father unless you are absolutely sure of its fruition. Take one day at a time.

Anna, 26 and a University of Virginia graduate, was in a physically abusive relationship and did not want the father of her twins involved in their lives. An inconclusive sexual-abuse charge against the same man in relation to an older daughter he had from a previous marriage made Anna all the more wary. For those reasons, she was willing to relieve her children's father of his financial responsibility toward them if he would leave them alone. "His history is such that given a certain amount of stress, I don't trust that he wouldn't physically or sexually abuse his children." Anna plans to file for a legal order for child support but will then make a verbal agreement not to collect if the biological father stays out of their lives. "If he's paying money, he is more than likely to come back and visit as a punishment to me," she concludes. "He's even threatened me, saying, `If you go for support, I'm gonna be involved in their lives.'"

Mothers who are ambivalent about the biological father's involvement usually feel that way because they don't believe the father will make a long-term commitment to his child. One such woman is Jocelyn, a 23-year-old legal secretary in New

York City and the mother of 13-month-old Caitlin. "I wouldn't mind if he saw her if he was going to be in her life full-force," she says, "but he is the type of person who would see her when he feels like it, and that's not fair to her—to have someone popping into her life once a year."

Some women don't tell fathers about their biological offspring. In years to come, a child in such a situation may resent his mother for having made such a conscious decision to rob both him and his father of a relationship. Unless the father poses a real danger to the child, you should inform him about his child and extend an offer of a relationship.

Facilitating a Relationship

Unless your child's father is dangerous to him or to you, invite him to take part in his child's life. Allow your child to grow up knowing who he is. If the father chooses not to participate, at least you'll know that you've done all you can. The burden of explaining the father's choice to the child, if the child becomes curious someday, will then be upon the father, rather than you.

Extend at least one invitation to participate in your child's life in writing; keep a copy for your child. I was shocked during a visitation hearing when Steve, my daughter's father, responded to a judge's question as to where he had been for the first four years of Morgan's life by claiming that he had "been kept" from her. I had extended a verbal invitation to Steve and his parents years before, and I had never imagined that he might deny this fact.

Denial and blame often play major roles in domestic disputes. And while my attorney was able to discredit Steve's claim by asking him to detail what steps he had taken to see his child, I quickly learned the importance of written documents. Written documents help judges and children separate fact from fiction.

Very often, when paternal grandparents take an interest in their grandchild, a father feels obligated to do the same. As I mentioned in an earlier chapter, I had agonized over whether to inform Steve's mother about Morgan. After four years, Steve had still not told her. Tragically, she was killed in a fall within her own home and died never knowing that she was a grandmother.

I felt strongly that Steve's mother should have been offered the choice of a relationship with her granddaughter; it should have been up to her to decide whether she would be part of her granddaughter's life. Steve and I disagreed adamantly about this matter. He claimed, "It would break her heart." I wondered, however, if he shied away from telling her about Morgan because he feared she would pressure him to allow her to visit her granddaughter. I ended up going along with his wishes not to tell his mother, however, because I did not want to interfere in the relationship between the two of them.

But by not telling his mother about Morgan, Steve was making the decision that she would not be involved with her granddaughter. After the death of his mother, Steve told me that his father was preparing to file a motion asserting his right to see Morgan and utilize visitation in another state. That was the last straw. I had made verbal and written offers to the paternal grandfather through his son.

I realized the picture Steve was trying to paint in court documents, and I felt forced to extend another invitation to Steve's father regarding a meeting with his granddaughter, but this one needed to be sent to him directly. I sent a brief, businesslike invitation that was about two sentences long. The letter merely told Steve's father that filing a motion was unnecessary. Contrary to what he may have been told, I had extended, through his son, an open invitation for him to meet his granddaughter, and welcomed the chance to introduce the two of them. We have yet to hear from him.

Neither in nor Out

A few fathers disappear for months or years on end. Psychologists refer to these fathers as absentee or uninvolved parents. I like to refer to them as "irregular" (though sometimes "negligent" seems a more appropriate description).

Beware the biological father who surfaces several years later and proclaims a need to see his unknown child.

Question the child's father extensively and determine his motives, sincerity and commitment. If you've created a healthy, stable environment and your child is well adjusted to the family circumstances, you may feel forced to take a great risk. But biological fathers have visitation rights. And you don't want to deny your child a potentially healthy relationship with his father.

Go to a law library or meet with an attorney to familiarize yourself with your jurisdiction's visitation laws and guidelines. Proceed cautiously and maintain a positive attitude. But be careful not to set your child up for a fall.

When Steve and I met one spring night to discuss the possibility of his taking an active part in Morgan's life, I was excited but cautious. To me, he seemed overly concerned about the logistics of shuttling her back and forth, where the two of us would live in five years and what would happen when we married other parties. I told Steve that I did not have all the answers to those questions and thought that we should take things one day at a time.

I asked him to think through his desire to participate in Morgan's life. "This isn't something you should walk into and then walk away from. That would be painful for her," I said. I didn't hear again from Steve on the issue until two years later, when the issue of child support arose. It was funny, though, because a recurring daydream had prepared me for this possibility.

In my vision, Morgan and I were at the zoo, in front of the elephant house, peering through the black vertical bars, awaiting "the meeting" at our designated point. I was looking at my watch and saying to myself, "It's 2:15, well past the agreed-upon time. Where is he?" Morgan was tugging on my wrist, eager to go see the other animals, and it was ludicrous to expect her to stand there any longer.

My experience with Morgan's father taught me that it's wise not to breathe a word to your child about the possibility of seeing his father until you see the tips of the man's tennis shoes (or loafers). I realize that sounds a little extreme, but you would be amazed at how many men have said they wanted to meet their children and never made concrete arrangements or physically appeared.

Jocelyn had a similar experience with her child's father. "He called for two weeks and said he wanted to see his child. I made an appointment for them to meet, and he called to cancel because he said he was sick." Jocelyn hasn't heard from the father regarding the issue since.

According to Tom Roberts, a family researcher and counselor at Western Kentucky University, a paternal relationship "that is interrupted or unsteady...can be more damaging for the child than not having the relationship at all."

With this pattern, the child may take the lack of commitment to the relationship personally and feel "that he is not liked by the father or that he did something wrong," explains Roberts. Share this concern with your child's father and consult with professionals if necessary.

Avoiding an Awkward Introduction

The issue of what to call the biological father requires some thought. The answer usually depends on his level of involvement with the child from the beginning.

Most women want their child's father to be "Daddy," but if time passes and the natural father has not been involved, they might ask themselves how long they should reserve the title. When I initially offered a relationship with my daughter to Steve when she was an infant, I fully expected that he would be called Daddy. But before they actually met a few years later,

I consulted with child psychiatrists. Morgan was four years old by then, and I was uncomfortable bestowing the title on her father because I did not sense a sincere desire to build a lasting relationship with my daughter. For example, he never asked questions about her health, when she began walking and talking, what activities and toys she liked and how she was doing in school. Even more telling was that he never even asked to see pictures of her. I also felt certain that I would marry and that my husband would assume the title and role of "Daddy," given Steve's past behavior. The professionals I met with recommended that I give Morgan the choice of what she would like to call her biological father, rather than tell her what to call him.

Before their meeting, Morgan and I had an impromptu conversation about the man she would see at the playground the next day. "His name is Steve and he's your father. He helped make you," I told her. "You can call him Steve, Dad or Daddy. Even if you decide to call him one thing now, you are always welcome to change your mind down the road. It's your choice," I stressed.

"Not yours," declared Morgan , confirming her understanding.

"Right," I responded.

At the pet farm during Morgan's second visit with her father, it finally became apparent what she would call him. He was relaxing on a picnic table and she was across the playground on a swing. She was ready for a push and decided that her father should be the one to help. "Steeeeeeve," Morgan hollered across the playground.

I've met many other mothers who refer to the fathers of their children by first name or as "Suzy's father." Most family professionals support that rationale. "A man who has not acted like a parent is not a father," says one psychologist. "'Daddy' and 'Father' are titles that should be earned."

Jocelyn feels the same way. The father of her daughter didn't come around, and Jocelyn's boyfriend became "Daddy" to little Caitlin. "She cries when he leaves now," says Jocelyn. But unless marriage is imminent, neither is this a good idea. If the relationship fails, the child who was misled could be confused over the role of the boyfriend and the meaning of "Daddy." The ramifications could be deep.

Father figures have even fought for their rights in court. One such case occurred in California a few years ago between a homosexual friend and the woman whose daughter he helped nurture. He celebrated the infant's momentous occasions and took care of the toddler regularly on weekends when the mother worked. The child called the man "Daddy" and gave him Father's Day cards.

When the friendship between the mother and the friend soured, the man filed for visitation and partial custody. Though not a biological parent, the man won his case based upon the argument that a parent is not necessarily biological but one who provides nurturing—the one whom the child believes to be "Daddy." "If the child believes, then the court should believe," argued the man's attorney. After the initial hearing, the mother tried to flee the country with her daughter and eventually lost all rights to her child, who is now being raised with her "daddy" and his male lover.

Child-Resistant Fathers

Some fathers never express an interest in their children. By a child's first birthday, if the father hasn't appeared, a mother who had hoped for such contact may suffer a mild depression. The second birthday can be just as difficult.

What could possibly be a legitimate explanation for a father's lack of involvement with his child? you may ask yourself. Anger toward the mother, a cramping of style, lack of money or time and a desire "not to interfere" are popular excuses for the lack of steady contact with a child.

But the reality behind an uninvolved father "is that he doesn't want the responsibility," says Marianne Walters, a family therapist in Washington, D.C. Many women have a hard time accepting a father's lack of interest in his biological child.

In the book *How to Attract Anyone, Anytime, Anyplace,* coauthors Susan Rubin and Barbara Lagowski give wonderful advice on how to deal with the pain of rejection:

1. **It's not personal**. The authors give the example of a woman who was turned down flat when she asked a man to dance. When he later approached her to apologize, she learned that the rejection signified not that she was too short or that her lipstick was smudged, but merely that he was hot and tired from a long, miserable ride on the expressway. He wanted to relax.

2. **It can be a favor**. In the case of a single pregnant woman abandoned by her child's father, the authors would view the quick adieu from Papa as a favor. "He didn't monopolize your time. He did you the favor by

turning you loose quickly, giving you a chance to get on with your life. Immediate turndowns are never setbacks. They're opportunities to move forward!"

3. **It's not serious.** "Meeting a special person always has been a numbers game. Single women have to work their way through a lot of nos before finding the right yes."

After you take stock of your assets and write down your achievements, talents and successes, the authors suggest an exercise that can help you stop worrying about what went wrong and start looking for something (or someone) better. Here is one, slightly revised, for single mothers.

1. It wasn't my fault because _____.

2. He misunderstood me because _____.

3. He isn't right for me (and my child) because _____.

4. I'm glad he said no (didn't propose) because _____.

5. I feel so good because _____.

6. I feel blessed because _____.

Rejection is a disappointment, but you can get over it if you set your mind to it. Everyone deserves to be loved, honored and cherished. If your child's father is not willing or able to offer that to you and your child, set your sights higher, on someone who will.

The Daddy Question and Self-Esteem

A child's questions about an uninvolved father are by far the hardest a mother will ever have to answer. I believe they are the most critical.

Some mothers of children with absent fathers have found that the "Daddy question" can come as early as when the child is two and a half. Others have found that the child never asks. In many instances, the question is triggered by direct inquiries from other children, such as "Where's your daddy?" or taunts such as "You don't have a daddy."

Most women are up-front in their responses to children's questions, says Walters. "But some women lie, particularly when there's a war on. The idea is that he died in a war. It's easier to tell your child that his father is dead." But generally the truth surfaces, she adds, and the trust once challenged may never be regained.

A few mothers count their lucky stars when the child doesn't ask about the family history, not realizing that it is a subject that they should bring up for their child's sake.

For most of us, however, the Daddy question will come, and we may wonder if we'll have the strength to answer it appropriately. Most psychologists agree that the subject of an uninvolved father or of parents who are not living together and not married should be discussed with the child. The conversation should be positive and appropriate to the child's age and understanding. If your child doesn't ask, you should look for an opportunity to talk about the family when he is between the ages of two and four, says Roberts. "If you notice that your son is particularly fond of another male, you could tie that in as an introduction to a conversation about his biological father, saying something like `I notice that you are awfully fond of so-and-so. Do you ever wonder about your father?'"

All of your conversations about your child's biological father should have positive overtones. Above all, your child should not feel personally at fault or to blame for the absence of a father. Your conversations are an opportunity for you to address any hurtful illusions your child may hold about himself and to build up his self-esteem.

In doing so, depersonalize the explanation as much as possible, advises Walters, who has counseled many single mothers. When you discuss with your child why you and his father aren't together or why he doesn't visit, she suggests some version of the statement "It has nothing to do with you; it has to do with your father and me and the relationship we had."

"Keep the explanation factual," says Emily Brown, a marriage and family therapist in Rosslyn, Virginia: "'We didn't get married because he has difficulties with relationships,' or 'he has difficulties with children.'"

The point to get across, concludes Roberts, is that the relationship between you and the child's father did not work out. That way, your child can rest assured that the father was not unhappy with him.

When Morgan, at age two and a half, started mentioning "Daddy" in virtually every sentence one afternoon, I thought it was something I needed to address. "Do you ever wonder about your daddy?" I asked.

"Yes," she responded.

"He lives in another city," I told her. "In Alexandria."

That was enough of a response for Morgan at that age, and, I believe, for any child under three. It was something tangible and something that she could repeat to others. When Morgan was four and ready for more of an explanation, I told her, "Your father and I did not get along well enough to get married. He knows how much I love you, and he thought it would be better for you to live with me."

As your child grows older, he may ask for more information about his father. In preparation for this very natural curiosity, save and share whatever information you have about the other parent, advises Brown.

"Questions about and a desire to search for the father are attempts to answer questions such as `Who am I? Why didn't he want me?'" says Roberts, who teaches parenting courses. "It's almost like checking out all that he's been told."

Be prepared to talk about the father when it's appropriate. "Even though you might prefer to say nothing and forget it all," says Brown, who has counseled many single mothers as well as adult children of singles, "your child needs to hear something about his father." Talk about subjects that offer insight into the father figure as a person, such as descriptions of what the father liked or disliked, says Brown. "You could say something like `Your father has beautiful eyes; he likes running' or `Your father never liked spinach,'" she suggests. The idea is to give your child a concrete image of his father.

Save photos or try to obtain pictures of the natural father and show them to your child, suggests Brown.

Regardless of your own feelings, says Walters, be positive in your representation of the father. But "don't make him out to be a hero," warns Roberts. Be careful not to build him up to be some mythological god. I believe too many children with absentee fathers buy into the myth that if their father had been around, life would have been glorious. "Don't use put-downs or pedestals," concludes Brown.

An acceptable statement about the father and his decision not to be involved might offer him the benefit of the doubt. "Your father did what he felt was best" is an example of how you could address such a question.

Obviously, "if the father is serving a jail sentence, you need not elaborate," says Roberts. Otherwise, "mention his name and perhaps the type of work he does or where he lives."

I was grateful for the insight of my friend Elizabeth, whose son, David, plays with my daughter. While the four of us were driving back from the National Zoo in Washington, D.C., one afternoon, Elizabeth shared a childhood episode that somehow indicated she did not know her father.

"Was your mother married when she had you?" I asked, my heart pounding. "No, she wasn't," replied Elizabeth, who went on to tell me that, indeed, she had grown up not knowing her natural father.

The children were sound asleep, and I had a million questions to ask. I felt as if I had stumbled upon a gold mine. Now, nearly two years after our first discussions on the subject, I often reflect on how our many conversations have eased my anxiety.

I learned that Elizabeth, now 35, was born to a single mother in the projects of Philadelphia. "I didn't realize that my family was different until I was five and was transferred to a Catholic school after my mother married," recalls the upbeat brunette. "For the first time, I noticed that everybody else had a mom *and* a dad."

Having an absent or inconsistent father is "something that causes one of two reactions," concludes Elizabeth. "It makes you say either 'Gosh, I feel like shit—my own father didn't want me,' or 'Hey, I'm wonderful. *He's* missing out.'" Elizabeth grew up believing the latter.

When Elizabeth asked her mother about the family history, she got little information. She remembers her mother saying, "Your father told me that he would never get married. And he never broke his promise. He doesn't like children, and he doesn't want a family." Elizabeth wanted to know more, but she had the distinct impression that her mother was not approachable on the subject. Because of the disapproval and discomfort she sensed from her mother, Elizabeth has no immediate plans to seek her father out, despite her curiosity about him.

Another worthwhile conversation to have with your child is one that focuses on families and how very different they are. Some families have a grandmother living with them; some don't have grandmothers at all. Others see an uncle only on Christmas and some have an uncle who drops by every weekend, perhaps to mow the lawn. Many families consider the family pet an essential member, be it a pug named Otis or, as in our case, a Himalayan named Olivia.

Above all, keep an open mind about your child's curiosity toward his biological father. Share information and photographs, if possible, that will help an absent father become a real person in your child's eyes. Don't attempt to stifle that interest.

Accepting the No-Show Daddy

Don't take the biological father's decision not to be involved personally. You may never quite understand his reasons, but it is important to accept his decision. The reason the lack of involvement is so hard to accept is that your child is missing out. You hurt for your child.

Many mothers waste valuable energy yearning for the day when a biological father will take an interest in his child. It may be necessary to mourn a lost dream before you move forward, but for your child's sake, it is important that you get over it. If you're having a difficult time working through the issue, consider getting help from a professional counselor.

Some men can't quite commit to the notion of fatherhood and yet have a strong curiosity about their offspring. They may wonder if the child looks like them. The mother may fantasize that if only the man would lay eyes on his child, he would instantly become attached to him or her. And sometimes this is exactly what happens. But not every father maintains a relationship with his child once he's quenched his curiosity. Remember that whether a relationship develops has nothing to do with the appeal of the child but rather with the father's readiness to handle the responsibility of a parent-child relationship.

Let Your Child's Best Interest Guide You

In talking with your child about his father, it is very important to avoid judgmental statements. The day will come when your child is grown and has established his own set of morals and priorities. As you answer whatever questions he or she has, be careful to allow your child to reflect on the situation and draw conclusions for himself.

My daughter, Morgan, seemed most appreciative of the photograph of her father that I was able to share with her shortly before they actually met. In order to prepare her, I told her nonchalantly, "We are going to the playground today. Your father might meet us there. He made you with Mommy and you might notice that he looks a lot like you. His name is Steve."

"Does he have blue eyes?" she inquired.

"Yes," I answered before offering her the snapshot her father had recently sent. It's one of a few photos of Steve that are now kept in a small album, along with pictures of the two of them together, in her bedroom bookcase, where she can see them whenever she likes.

The dynamics of any two families are never the same, so what works for one family may not work for another. In making any difficult decision about what's best for my child, I generally ask myself whether I will feel proud and comfortable about my decision in 5, 10 or 20 years?

It can be difficult to interact with the father; it can be equally as difficult to justify a father's absence. But if you remember that the choice you make is for your child's sake, you can muster strength and courage no matter how impossible the situation may seem.

Four

The Difference Child Support

Can Make

If the father of your child is less than overjoyed at the news of your pregnancy, you may hesitate to take such legal steps as filing for child support, establishing paternity and determining custody and visitation schedules. But don't.

Take a good hard look at your finances, the cost of day care and preschool and your living situation, and determine whether you really have a choice. Child support is your child's right. Even if you don't immediately need the money to provide a safe and comfortable life for your child, you could invest it in a college account or save it for your child's discretion later. Legally binding agreements with regard to the issues of paternity, custody and visitation are also in the long-term interest of your child, and they can resolve misunderstandings and eliminate a lot of mental anguish for yourself as well.

Life is unpredictable. Circumstances change. If you don't plan to take legal action now, at least learn about the ways in which the law provides for children who are not living with their biological fathers.

Courts and lawyers can be intimidating. You may not be sure if what you and your child are entitled to is worth the hassle. You may wonder if you even have enough money to hire an attorney; you may worry that if you did press your daughter's father for child support, he might retaliate. You may not even know where to begin.

For those reasons, this chapter starts by dispelling the myths and fallacies of family law issues for unmarried mothers. By knowing the facts about legislation and agreements common to parents with a child born outside of marriage, you will be able to negotiate on more realistic terms, put many of your fears to rest and avoid the mistakes often made by others.

Few mothers want to go to court. Instead, they may wait patiently for a father's voluntary offer of cash or fantasize about a surprise visit in which he bestows a carton of diapers and formula upon them. Unfortunately, however, many mothers are forced to battle a father for the monetary support of a child he helped create.

Here, you'll learn how to approach your child's father in a positive manner about family law issues and where he sees himself fitting into the life of his child. Even before a child support order can be awarded, you need to establish your child's paternity, a legal determination of who the father is. Often, that requires a blood test. In talking to the father, you may discover that he's perfectly willing to acknowledge paternity. If so, that's one legal motion you won't need to file.

Some mothers believe that such a legal determination is unnecessary. You may know who the child's father is and not want anything from him. But we'll spotlight the emotions of a young woman whose mother never bothered to legally determine who the father was. Choices of legal representation will be explored, as will the amount of money a mother can expect to be awarded.

In the second half of the chapter, we'll highlight additional financial matters, including legal documents, policies and preparations that single mothers must seek in order to secure their children's future and well-being. In looking at the importance of wills, trusts and life insurance for the single mother, you will learn about precautions unique to the unmarried mother, such as protecting your child's estate from the clutches of an estranged biological father.

Family Law Issues: Homework First

Before making a concrete decision to pursue any of your child's rights, educate yourself. You need to learn about typical rulings and agreements in family law cases similar to those in which you may be involved. Armed with such knowledge, you will know just how fair and realistic your positions are vis-à-vis your child's father.

The book *Mom's House, Dad's House: Making Shared Custody Work*, by Isolina Ricci, is a valuable tool and a good starting point. The book contains examples of parenting agreements and a master list of family law issues that you will need to discuss.

Another way of gathering information is to schedule a consultation with a family law attorney who will talk briefly to you about similar cases and estimate the amount of child support you are likely to be awarded.

If you are really ambitious, you could go to the public library and read through the family law section of your state's code. There you will find rulings and codes outlining the factors that influence the amount of child support, visitation and determination of custody.

Finally, if you know you're bound for court, sit in on related domestic law hearings. To do so, call the domestic relations division of your family law court and ask when cases involving child support, visitation and custody are heard. Witnessing hearings can clarify any misconceptions you might have and ease your tensions about legal proceedings that can't be resolved outside of the courtroom.

Knowledge Is Power: What Does He Want?

It helps to know what thoughts and emotions are dancing around inside the mind of your baby's father. If you are not in regular contact with him, invite him to meet with you for a talk, ideally in a public place, such as a restaurant or a park. If he's not willing to meet with you, try to get his position on the legal issues in a telephone conversation.

It would be beneficial to know, first of all, if he believes or is willing to admit that he is your baby's father. Is he comfortable with that fact and is he willing to assume some sort of responsibility for your child? Is he planning to be in the hospital when you give birth?

Your questions may fall on deaf ears, and you may not be able to progress even beyond these basic ones. In that case, give him some time. This is a heavy load for most single men to digest. Let him know how he can reach you if wants to get in touch with you over the next few months.

His actions may tell you a whole lot more than his words. If he's mum or you discover a disconnected telephone line, you can probably assume that he won't be your coach for Lamaze classes. He may flat out deny that he is the father of your child. If so, don't take it to heart. Most informed fathers, based upon the advice of attorneys, won't discuss any issues or acknowledge paternity without the confirmation of a blood test. In that case, hold your questions until after the test results are in. Many fathers are more than willing to talk at that point. Above all, maintain your dignity and don't harass him.

From Here to Paternity

Paternity, the legal determination as to who your child's father is, can be established in a number of ways. Some are voluntary; others are forced. Normally, a finding of paternity is required before child support, custody or visitation arrangements can be determined.

If you and your child's father are on friendly terms, you can simply ask him to sign your baby's birth certificate before a notary public. Related forms, available at some hospitals and in county juvenile and domestic relations courts, may be signed by fathers who are ready later to voluntarily and officially acknowledge their children.

Depending on state law, a father's verbal or written acknowledgment of a child as his own may be viewed as conclusive evidence of paternity. If the father does not participate in the birth or has become estranged, you may be forced to undergo blood tests and hearings to establish paternity. Normally the presumed father has a right to blood tests before a conclusive finding can be made that he is indeed the father.

After paternity is established, your child has the same legal rights as one born to a married couple. Among those rights are medical and social-security benefits, life insurance and, in some cases, intestate rights.

The Pluses of Establishing Paternity

You may not have given much thought to a legal determination of paternity. You know who the father is, you tell yourself, and you may not expect any financial contributions from him. But I believe it's crucial.

In all of your decisions, you need to reflect upon the long-term effect on the well-being of your child. "Paternity is a basic right of the child," points out Michael E. Barber, a family law attorney in Sacramento and former chairman of the American Bar Association's family law section. Barber tells his pregnant clients to start filling out paperwork for legal proceedings immediately.

In addition to financial benefits, there is your child's genetic heritage and his emotional ties to a father. "The inherent need to know one's roots is indefinable but a deep, natural compulsion," maintains Barber. Many adopted children and those born to an unknown parent seek them out later for information about the circumstances of the birth and answers to the question "Who am I?"

One young woman whose mother never got around to having paternity established will probably never solve the mystery of who her father is. Born to an unmarried mother, Tanya found herself again curious about her paternal side when she was 23 years old and about to give birth to her own child. "I only have half of a family tree," Tanya told me, expressing feelings similar to those of an adopted child.

The married man whom her mother identified as Tanya's father vehemently denied paternity and accused her mother of being crazy. He even brought an attorney and a stack of legal papers with him to the initial, brief encounter the two had when Tanya was 18 years old. Tanya's last-ditch attempt at age 23 to solve the mystery by writing a letter to the man requesting voluntary blood tests didn't even generate a response.

Since blood tests were never taken, Tanya will probably never know for sure who her father is. Because she is no longer a minor and therefore not eligible for support from her father, Barber explains, there is little she can do legally if the alleged father won't consent to blood tests. If Tanya were a minor, however, the court could compel him to undergo blood tests to determine whether she was eligible for his financial support.

Many women freeze when, just hours after their baby's birth, they are handed forms related to parents and the official birth certificate. Some let their emotions influence how they handle the document; they may feel that a father who is not supportive doesn't deserve to be acknowledged on the birth certificate.

But by not establishing paternity, you are forcing your child to go through life with a document that has a blank space where the father's name belongs. I can't believe, given that your child does in fact have a father, that he would be comfortable having a birth certificate with nothing written in the space for the father's name.

Laws in some states force mothers to leave the space blank unless the father consents to using his name. But once blood test results are conclusive, mothers can request a new birth certificate that bears the father's name. For your child's sake, establish paternity and determine legally where the other half of the child's roots lie.

Besides being beneficial for your child's mental well-being, "paternity is the gateway to the entire child support process," says Robert Harris, spokesman for the Office of Child Support Enforcement, U.S. Department of Health and Human Services. But be prepared: "Once it's established, the door swings open for the father's visitation rights and custody decisions."

Because paternity is a bridge to child support, many men request blood tests to determine without a doubt if they are the child's father. Some women are offended by the request, because they believe the men know from the nature of their intimate relationship that the child is theirs. They believe such a test implies fraud and promiscuity on their part, according to Barber. But Barber and other attorneys typically advise the alleged father to make such a request. Imagine paying out hundreds of thousands of dollars to support a child, only to find out years later that he or she is not yours. Imagine such a father denying himself the right to have other children in order to meet this child's needs.

Without the father's voluntary acknowledgment of paternity, a mother can establish it by going to court with a lawyer or a representative from the state child support enforcement office. The final option is to file paperwork on your own case. Call the juvenile and domestic relations court in your jurisdiction. Find out if there are intake officers who can help you fill out the paperwork, or examples of motions on hand so that you can fill in the blanks of your own legal papers based on them. If your child's father challenges or denies paternity in court, the judge can issue an order requiring blood tests.

Feeling Woozy? The Low-down on Paternity Tests

Just the thought of blood tests has prevented many a mother from establishing paternity. Many fathers are aware of this fear and use it as a weapon, threatening to make a mother and her baby go through a myriad of blood tests. It's a challenge to get beyond the mental humiliation of the paternity tests. It helps to think rationally and practically about the issue, like a businessman, rather than emotionally. Is a prick in the arm and a day in court worth an additional $300 to $800 a month? Probably so. Remind yourself that you are doing this for your child.

By the end of the spring day during which Morgan and I had paternity tests, I could look back and laugh at my unnecessary paranoia as we strolled into her school, late from "a doctor's appointment." Both of us wore Band-Aids on our arms;

hers was decorated with Snoopy characters. I felt certain that our adhesive strips, strategically placed, were dead giveaways to our private battles. They screamed "paternity tests."

If blood tests are ordered by the court, you will probably be sent to a local clinic to have your blood drawn. Some courthouses have a facility for this procedure on the premises. Adults and toddlers are usually pricked in the arm, an infant in the leg or foot. The samples are usually tested for a battery of genetic markers, including DNA, which is 99 percent accurate, says Barber, who also has worked extensively on the parentage testing committee of the American Association of Blood Banks. The results often are mailed to both parties and the court within a few weeks.

The blood tests usually cost $100 to $300 per person when court-ordered, and the father is often required to pay for the tests if they were done at his request. In some jurisdictions, the cost of the tests is split equally. Normally, the mother must reimburse the man if the tests determine that he is not the father. The tests are generally more expensive when administered without a court order.

It is common procedure in some jurisdictions for you and the alleged father to be tested at the clinic at the same time. For court records and for the purpose of verifying the identity of those tested, you may be asked to pose for a family snapshot. If you fear hostility during a face-to-face encounter with your child's father, you may want to telephone the courthouse or the clinic to reschedule your appointment for a time when he won't be there. In the heat of legal motions flying back and forth, I feared that ours would have been a nasty encounter, so I phoned ahead and changed my appointment.

Additionally, I was uneasy about the prospect that the blood tests would be the backdrop for the introduction of my four-year-old daughter and her father. I did not want him to see her in such a vulnerable position. It was too easy and too down-and-dirty; I felt that if he wanted to see her, it should be more dignified. It should not be something required or forced upon him by the court; he should have to go out of his way.

As far as my daughter's father knew, we were scheduled to be tested with him. When Morgan and I arrived, the clinic personnel told me that Steve, who had been tested earlier, paced back and forth and got up out of his seat several times to approach them, asking, "Where is she?" They said that he had waited for a half hour in his car outside the clinic after he was done.

Once tests have confirmed paternity, call your state's division of vital records to inquire about procedures for issuance of a new birth certificate. When I called Virginia's Division of Vital Records about adding the name of Morgan's father, I was asked to provide a copy of the court order regarding paternity results, information surrounding the birth and various facts about her father, including the date and place of his birth. The new birth certificate cost five dollars.

Paternity's Link to Your Child's Last Name

In some states, paternity may be linked to the last name you are able to give your child. Many mothers at least toy with the option of using the biological father's last name for their child. For some, it is a highly charged emotional issue, with fathers trying to exert control over the situation by either insisting on the use of their last name or prohibiting it. Mothers sometimes get a sense of satisfaction in using their own names and thus snubbing a father. Ultimately, the decision will probably hinge not on which combination of names has the best cadence but rather on the status of the relationship between the two parents and, more importantly, the expected level of involvement between your baby and his father. I gave Morgan my last name. I felt certain that her father would not be involved in her life, and I did not want to subject her to a last name to which she could not even attach a face.

Christina, a 25-year-old comptroller for a software company, gave her son her own last name as well. Though her son's father had proposed to her just a month before she became pregnant, during her pregnancy he packed up his belongings and moved to an island resort 10 hours away. "As far as I know, I will be raising my child alone. I'm not trying to make a personal statement that it's *my* baby," explains Christina, who had dated the man for four years. "I just feel it would be less complicated if the child has my name."

Another mother, Renee, "didn't even consider" giving her daughter the last name of her biological father. "I think it's psychologically detrimental to give her the name of a person who doesn't want anything to do with her," she explained. Other mothers have made the same choice after being deserted by the father during pregnancy. They don't think the father in these cases deserves to have a child named after him.

But Lisa, who will soon marry, is reconsidering the issue of last names; her son, Justin, has hers, but the toddler's biological father and his wife are very involved in his life. Lisa plans to take her fiancé's last name, and she wants to have more children. "All of us but Justin will have the same last name. I'm wondering now if my son should have his father's name."

Some states have laws regarding the last names that mothers are able to give their babies without the father's consent. In Virginia, for example, a law passed in 1991 allows unmarried mothers to give the child the father's last name on a birth certificate without conclusive testing if the father signs a form in front of a witness. "If he doesn't sign the form, it's not allowed," says Margery Huge, spokeswoman for Arlington Hospital in Virginia. In other states, a mother can virtually pick a last name out of a hat. Call the maternity ward at a hospital in your area or your state's bar association to find out the laws regarding last names for your child.

Upon reflection, I am grateful to have had the paternity tests and an official document declaring without a shadow of a doubt exactly who my daughter's father is. For me, it attested to the fact that Morgan was born to two parents.

Child Support: To Seek or Not

A child with parents living in two different households is entitled to child support—a monthly sum of money sent from one parent to the other for expenses related to raising and caring for their child. Some people believe child support is a benefit that comes only with marriage. Not so. A child born to a single parent is just as entitled to financial support as one who was born to married parents who later divorced.

Spousal support, of course, is a different story. In an instance where the mother has been receiving Aid for Dependent Children, the support awarded will initially go to reimburse the support advanced by the public.

The age to which a parent pays support for his child varies from state to state. Generally it is until the child is of majority age—18 or 21 years old in most cases. Some state laws require a parent to provide for college education.

For the parties involved, the issue of child support is often highly emotional. Guilt over an accidental pregnancy, personal pride, fear about how the father might react if forced to pay child support, the father's accusations about being "trapped"—all these may influence personal decisions about the pursuit of child support.

But the court isn't influenced by personal feelings or circumstances. A judge does not differentiate between a child conceived in a one-night stand and one that results from a long-term affair or marriage. The court sees a child in need of financial provisions and, in making its decision, considers only salaries, living and health-care expenses, and child care or school expenses.

There is little question that it is easier to raise a child when both parents contribute financial support. It's more comforting to ponder which educational program or facility would better suit your toddler than to fret over whether you can afford the school's supplies.

In deciding whether to seek child support, consider some financial facts. A woman who may be entitled to $600 a month for child support and does not file for a legal order requiring the father to pay is actually forfeiting at least $151,200, if her state awards payments until age 21. And that figure does not account for orders that may be submitted to increase the amount of support because of inflation or raises in salary.

On the advice of an attorney, Lisa began legal proceedings just three months into her pregnancy. When her son's father would not acknowledge paternity before blood tests, Lisa requested prenatal blood tests, which were denied by the court. At her son's birth, however, she had blood drawn from the umbilical cord, to get an order for child support payments as quickly as possible.

On the more than $1,000 Lisa receives each month from her son's father, a surgeon, she was able to spend two years at home with her child before returning to nursing school. "I think Don was put off in the beginning, upset and scared. But he fell in love with our son and his whole attitude changed."

Although the father of Lisa's child was forthcoming with money after paternity tests, Lisa says she believes that "in the end it's good that men are forced to pay, because it takes away some of their guilt about not raising their child."

"Raising a child is so expensive," says Nancy, who recently was awarded $300 a month in support from her daughter's father. "A child deserves a life that is good, and that comes with money, unfortunately," states Nancy, 40, who is working toward a master's degree in social work at Gallaudet University and credits child support with being the reason she is able to work only part-time and therefore spend more time with her daughter.

For Renee, 30, "support was a financial necessity." She uses every penny of the $780 a month she was awarded, and more, to pay the $200 a week required for her daughter's nanny.

A few of the mothers who don't seek support forfeit that right in an effort to keep an abusive father away from their child. Others are financially secure women in their late thirties and early forties, many of whom had sexual relations with the purpose of getting pregnant. These mothers are often not interested in future dealings with their lover. They offset some of their guilt by not seeking child support.

Diane, 37, waived her legal right to child support and moved in with her mother because she so feared the request for money would act as a catalyst to visitation. "I thought that if I asked him for child support, he would visit my son purely out of revenge," says Diane, an accounting administrator for a steel firm in Houston. "Ten years down the road, I didn't want him coming back and asking me for visitation." So she asked the father to sign a waiver relinquishing his parental rights (a legal option in Texas, although not all states), and he did.

Dollars and Sense: What's My Child Entitled To?

Before you commit yourself to the infantry and the cause, you will probably want to know exactly what you're fighting for. The amount of child support that a father will be required to pay each month is derived primarily from both parents' income. Other factors, such as outstanding loan obligations, cash flow from property, other children, medical costs, day-care needs and extraordinary medical costs also are considered.

Most states allow the father to write and send the checks on his own accord. If over time his checks are typically late or do not even arrive, the court can order automatic wage withholding from his paycheck. The federal government is now moving to require automatic wage withholding in most cases. State laws allow for additional enforcement techniques, such as the confiscation of a delinquent father's state and federal income-tax refunds, liens on real estate and the seizure and sale of property to pay past-due support.

To figure out how much support Steve should pay me each month, my attorney looked at my income at the time, $25,000, and his income, $40,000. He also considered additional health insurance payments of $8 a month for Morgan to be on my policy, child-care expenses of about $750 per month and outstanding extraordinary medical expenses of $30 a month from Morgan's premature birth.

Given these variables, in Virginia, the monthly child support payment Steve was required to pay fell somewhere between $800 and $1,000 a month, depending on whose lawyer was doing the calculations and how the lawyer guessed the judge would rule on certain variables. Some issues are left to the judge's discretion after the attorneys present their cases. Most attorneys strive to settle matters outside the courtroom, literally, and even pass offers back and forth while sitting on the benches outside the judge's chambers. But Steve and I were unable to reach an agreement on the issues of whether the entire cost of a private education was justifiable as I was claiming, who would be entitled to Morgan as a tax deduction and whether money related to the deduction should be considered additional income for me.

The judge determined that I, as custodial parent, should be entitled to the full tax advantage for Morgan—in other words that I should be able to claim her as a dependent. He would not count the tax deduction as additional income. But the judge apparently thought that private school was not a necessity but a personal choice. In his factoring of child support, he used the average cost of area schools and child care—$400 a month based upon research by Steve and me—rather than the entire monthly cost, $750, of her school.

In a California case in which both parents were making $50,000 and child-care costs were $800 a month, Barber figured the support payment of a father to be $1,000 per month, assuming the father rarely visits the child. A father who visits every other weekend and some holidays receives a reduced rate of support in California—in this case $850 per month. The assumption is that the father who visits regularly is taking care of some of the child's fixed costs. Likewise, in that state, if the father has the child 50 percent of the time, the support rate is reduced to $377.

Charts that represent the state's guidelines on child support can be found in most public libraries in the state's code. But additional factors, such as how much money to allot for a private day-care center that may be more expensive than the average child-care center, are at a judge's discretion. Therefore, family law attorneys often calculate a variety of figures on child support.

Drama in the Court

If you proceed legally with a motion for child support, prepare to see a side of your child's father that you never knew existed. Some fathers and attorneys may employ tactics to delay blood tests or question the validity of them. Others may try to pay you off. A father's counsel might also question the prior sex life of the mother. "It's a legitimate area of inquiry," Barber says. "But generally I tell my fathers to be prepared to reach deep into their pockets."

Charlene amicably approached the father of her son, Holden, when asking for a little money every now and then to help pay for the baby's staples, such as diapers and formula. But "he always claimed he never had any," says Charlene, who had hoped she would not have to resort to legal action but felt forced to seek a legal order when a patient and reasonable approach didn't work.

In court, the father's attempt to further delay paying support backfired. "My client has not been properly served," the father's lawyer told the judge. The judge looked at the notice of service and replied, "If he's not here today I'll issue a bench warrant for his arrest." The attorney then stated that he thought he could find the son's father. He went outside the courtroom, and in walked the father. Charlene noticed that everyone in the courtroom laughed, with the exception of the judge. He ordered the father to pay Charlene's legal bills.

When Steve challenged paternity, I knew that it was a common reaction and didn't take it personally. I was grateful for the temporary support agreement, a little-known option that my attorney, Richard M. Wexell, fought for when he learned that Steve would challenge paternity and thus delay the onset of actual child support payments. The temporary agreement stated that Steve would begin paying support immediately and that I would repay every penny to him in the event that the test concluded he was not Morgan's father.

Since we had not yet determined the amount of support in a hearing and would not do so until after the blood tests, the attorneys reached an agreement in which Steve paid temporary support in an amount between the two estimates calculated by our attorneys. These payments would continue until the next hearing, during which we would review blood test results and, if conclusive, determine the exact amount of support. Our agreement also stated that Steve would be required to make back payments if the figure we settled upon in court was higher than the temporary figure. Because of the temporary order, I was able to leave the courthouse with a check that day.

A desperate man might resort to threats against the woman or her child. "Threats should be taken seriously, but that doesn't mean you should knuckle under to them," Barber says. Report threats to a law enforcement agency and ensure they're on record. "If a woman is harmed and there is something on the record indicating hostility from a former lover, the father of the child will then be a prime suspect," Barber says. "Thus, a man who recklessly makes hostile statements mortgages his right to be presumed innocent if his child or the mother is ever injured under unexplained circumstances."

The decision to proceed with legal actions after life-threatening statements is difficult. You will probably question the father's motives and how well you actually know him. Barber finds men who threaten or try to persuade the other party that they may cheat them out of support to be a certain breed who rebel against the control. "Most of them are just taking the bad-guy approach. If the threats or tactics work once, they'll keep it up," he says.

If you encounter threats or inappropriate statements, consult with domestic violence specialists within the child support enforcement office, your local police station or the juvenile and domestic relations court. "Let the threatening party know you have taken this step," advises Barber. "Your best defense is a good offense."

When an Order Isn't Enough

Of course, it's not always as easy as filing a motion and obtaining a court order to collect child support. A court order is not a guarantee that a support check will end up in your mailbox on time. But this decade's campaign about "deadbeat dads" has resulted in a cottage industry of private collection agencies, media campaigns and legislation requiring new employee reports that make it more difficult for fathers to avoid paying.

Fortunately, you will still have a few methods of recourse for fathers who ignore legal orders.

AUTOMATIC WAGE WITHHOLDING

If a child support payment is more than 30 days late, you can return to court to request automatic wage withholding.

This legal step is best for fathers who have been with an employer longer than a year and who do not change jobs frequently.

Such a motion usually requires another hearing that gives the father an opportunity to explain why he hasn't been paying his child support on time. If the judge determines that he has been negligent, automatic wage withholding will be ordered. If assigned, you will be paid child support directly from the father's employer. Like checks that are automatically deposited or payments that are automatically withdrawn, the portion that's your child support will not even appear on the father's paycheck. This method is becoming more prevalent. Not seeing the money in a paycheck or having to write a monthly check can ease the sting that an angry father may feel each month.

PRIVATE COLLECTION AGENCIES

Another alternative is a private collection agency. The agencies, which use the tactics of private detectives, often are enlisted to collect from men who flee across state lines to avoid child support. The agencies charge the client only if they recover money from the father.

Dennis Bannon, the owner of such an agency in Laurel, Maryland, has handled hundreds of such cases. "I work with a sense of urgency," Bannon says. "The average recovery time is between 10 minutes and one month." Bannon takes 25 percent of the money that is recovered.

Mothers dealing with difficult cases might want to consult with a representative at one of the largest of these collection agencies, Find Dad, by calling 1-800-PAY-MOMS.

But Barber warns against hiring such an agency before conclusive evidence of paternity has been established. "You have no basis for action on their part until you have a judgment of parentage or a support order. You could find yourself in deep trouble if you hired a collection agency to find the supposed father. You don't want to be hit with a lawsuit for harassment."

Those who don't plan to legally file for child support today need to realize that circumstances change and individuals change. "Someone who is cooperative today may not be in the future," warns Robert Harris, spokesman for the office of child support enforcement, U.S. Department of Health and Human Services, who suggests looking at support over the lifetime of the child. "You may be able to provide today, but will you be able tomorrow?"

Child support makes men accountable for their children. I've heard numerous adult children of divorced parents tell me with an "Are you kidding?" attitude that their father never contributed financially after he departed the family or the relationship.

Child support payments, parlayed into something tangible, such as a new home or a private education, give children a concrete reason to be grateful to their fathers, even those who may not be physically present in their lives. Furthermore, no mother wants her child to grow up with bitter thoughts of his father. One who pays child support will be more worthy of his child's respect.

Custody and Visitation

As soon as paternity has been established, you should file a legal document related to the custody of your child. Visitation schedules, if the father desires to see his child, and the determination of custody are matters that are often presented during the same hearing. If a couple cannot agree on such issues as who will be the legal custodian of the child and how often and for how long the baby's father can visit his child, a judge may ultimately need to make a legal determination.

Practically speaking, a legal determination of the two issues makes sense. A visitation order can clarify expectations and alleviate stress and anguish over such issues as how to handle missed visits and tardiness. For security reasons, most schools and day-care centers these days ask parents to fill out paperwork that includes a question about custody of children. I was required by my daughter's school to bring in a copy of the court order stating that I am the sole custodial parent for Morgan. Other mothers are halted during the application process if they cannot prove that they have custody of their child.

It is not uncommon for a father to start inquiring about visitation and custody when a mother expresses or takes steps to seek child support. As a few desperate fathers see it, therein lies their bargaining power or trump card. It's not unusual for a father's threats to include warnings about taking the child away or suing for custody. Such talk may flow freely even though the father has never held his baby.

Soon after I filed for child support, my daughter's father shared a future vision saturated with his visitation time. Christmas and summer months would all be his with Morgan, he informed me ambitiously, even though she was nearing age four and he had not yet taken the initiative to meet her. If this type of retaliation is your fear, don't panic without knowing the facts.

Instead, educate yourself about realistic arrangements and court orders in other situations like yours before proceeding. You may also contact your state child-support enforcement office and request written materials that provide answers to many basic questions, often in a question-and-answer format. This, and the following real-life situations detailed in this book, will help you know exactly which emotional reactions are common and what actions are within the realm of legal possibilities.

Your decision may boil down to somewhat of a gamble. You may find yourself wondering, as I did, whether your baby's father will really devote himself to the child or simply use visitation time as a way of getting back at you? Or is either scenario unlikely given his reluctance to give up such personal freedoms as the ability to travel and socialize at will?

I felt greatly relieved when an attorney told me that he thought it was highly unlikely that my daughter's father could come in off of the street, literally as a stranger, and expect to be with our four-year-old child alone. He *was* a stranger, and his visits would have to start slowly and with supervision. For that reason, I knew that holidays and summer vacations would be a long time coming. But if Morgan's father truly wanted to share his life and love with her, who was I to object?

With that rationale, I decided to proceed, in spite of Steve's warnings, with a child support motion. Steve, as predicted, did move to get a visitation order. But my hunch about visitation not being a heartfelt desire may have been right. Although he was awarded between two and four hours of supervised visitation every other Sunday, Steve racked up only seven hours the first year. But I am grateful that the two were at least able to meet. Raising children is hard enough for those who are committed to the task; it's an even taller order for someone to devote himself to the expense and time associated with visitation just for spite.

If you and your child's father are amicable and he has been involved with the birth and expressed a desire to be involved in the upbringing of your child, try talking through the choices of partial or joint custody, which divides the legal responsibility of the child equally between the two of you.

Most mothers with an uninvolved father file for sole custody. If you are awarded sole custody, you will be entitled to make major decisions for your child on your own, such as whether he will be circumcised, what religion he will be raised in or whether he will be baptized, which day-care or elementary school he will attend, or whether a major medical procedure will be administered. Joint custody of a child means that major decisions throughout the child's life should be shared, requiring consultations on those issues.

If there has been some hostility between you and your baby's father, it's important to file for sole custody soon after the birth, warns Barber, "to get control of the case, prevent child snatching and make sure that your legal rights to the child are exclusive to the degree that the facts of the case permit."

Many mothers make the mistake of not filing for custody because they don't anticipate that their child's father will ever come around. But Barber advises against this. "File for sole custody in order to protect yourself in the event the child is stolen [by the father]." It does happen on occasion.

Barber offers this example of a typical problem scenario that could arise if custody has not been established: "A father takes the child into his home after birth; the mother lives there too. Father holds the child out to his neighbors and says, `Hey, look at my baby.'" The relationship wanes and the woman moves out. The mother has never firmed up her rights for legal or sole custody. "At best, the mother will be caught up in a legal tussle. At worst, the father comes over with his brother-in-law, snatches the child, and they march off to Canada. There is not much she could do right away. As the law sees it, the child is with his father. Without a legal determination of custody, the law views the rights of both parents as equal. If the mother did have sole custody, however, she could have officials standing at the border." Read through the section below on legal representation to determine which route toward a binding agreement suits your needs.

Daddy's Days: Visitation Schedules

If the father of your child has expressed an interest in regular meetings and outings with his offspring, you may want to consider solidifying a schedule of regular visits. With a legal agreement regarding visitation, both parties are more apt to take the arrangements seriously.

Visitation arrangements can vary from supervised outings every other weekend and weeknight dinners to entire summers and/or alternating holidays, depending on the devotion, proximity and preferences of the parents. In *Mom's House, Dad's House*, author Isolina Ricci states that fathers usually are awarded "reasonable visitation." But because the term is so vague and its interpretation so vast, Ricci suggests an explicit agreement that determines the exact hours of the visits, how often they will occur and the rigidity of the schedule, arrangements for the exchange of the child, and consequences in the event that the father is tardy or does not want to exercise his right of visitation.

In California, most custody and visitation arrangements, according to Barber, allow for the mother to be the sole custodian and give the father between 10 percent and 30 percent visitation time. "Most often, that means the father has the child on weekends and one night a week for dinner. But that usual pattern of joint legal custody for divorced parents does not hold true for unmarried parents, where more often the mother has sole custody due to the father's lack of bonding and true desire to be involved."

Standard visitation for a father in Iowa means the child would stay overnight with the father every other weekend, half of all of the major holidays and one month each summer, according to Jennifer Rose, an attorney in private practice in Shenandoah, Iowa, and former chairman of the family law section of the state bar association.

Of course, just because a visitation order has been made doesn't necessarily mean that the father will adhere to its guidelines, Barber points out. You may find that "the father does not arrive on time to pick up the child or he does not bring the child back on time; perhaps because of a new love interest he's skipped a couple weekends of visitation," Barber says. "Or maybe the mother is not at home with the children when he comes to pick them up."

If your child's father consistently or drastically departs from the agreement, you may have to decide whether the best possible outcome warrants the anguish and expense of returning to court. Again, explore related cases and consult an attorney before filing any paperwork.

In California, the law provides penalties for failing to keep up with visitation as scheduled. For instance, the father may be required to pay for baby-sitting costs if the mother was forced to forfeit plans made for the time he was scheduled to visit. In other states, he may simply get the equivalent of a verbal scolding. Scenarios such as those detailed above typically lead to anger and frustration on the part of the parents and the couples do occasionally go back to court to have a new order drawn up.

A Final Word of Caution

Disgruntled parents are involved in a startlingly high number of kidnapping cases. A study by the National Center for Missing and Exploited Children concluded that 42 percent of all child abductions were committed by a former husband or boyfriend; an additional 21 percent involved a current husband or boyfriend.

Knowing this, I have taken precautions, and you should too. Have your child fingerprinted and make a videotape of him once a year. You can usually get the prints done at your local police department, the sheriff's office or at the county fair, where the local law enforcement office often sets up an information booth. And don't feel guilty or paranoid. You're just being smart. These are steps that any responsible parent, regardless of marital status, should take as well.

The Great Divide: Getting to a Legal Agreement

If you've decided to seek legally binding agreements with regard to your child's rights but are still hoping to avoid the cost and hostility that can sometimes result from legal proceedings, you might consider negotiation and mediation as an alternative to going before the gavel.

Many mothers find that after paternity has been established, the father is more willing to talk outside of the courtroom. Fathers often become more interested in meeting with mothers personally after they've been served notice of a court hearing to determine legal matters such as child support or custody. In fact, don't be surprised if shortly after receiving such a legal notice, your child's father calls you to request a personal meeting and negotiation outside of court.

Negotiation and Mediators

If you are able to meet with your child's father personally, try to hold the encounter to a fixed agenda. Remember which issues you are trying to resolve. Judges like it when couples try to work things out among themselves before asking the court to settle matters. With that in mind, you will want to let your child's father know in writing that you are willing to discuss issues, but if the matter is not resolved by a certain date, you will be forced to file a motion before the court.

Successful mediation between parents, according to Ricci, may require that the two of you relate to each other in a new way, one that is less intimate and more businesslike. Ricci describes this relationship as one in which both parties invest little emotion and keep personal remarks on the level that exists between two business acquaintances. For example, "if the [neighborhood] druggist asks how you are, you answer, `Just fine, thank you,' even if you have had a miserable day," Ricci points out. Formal courtesies, public meetings, explicit agreements, contracts and structured meetings are also the norm for business relationships.

Try to keep the conversation focused on those issues involving the rights of your child that you are hoping to resolve. You may need to begin by asking your child's father how he feels about certain responsibilities. How does he feel with regard to the financial and emotional support of your child? Is he willing to voluntarily contribute money regularly to help ease the basic costs of rearing your child? Is so, how much does he think he can comfortably contribute, and when can he begin?

Depending on how well he's holding up, you may want to address the issue of his relationship with the child and what you can expect from him. He may still be confused about the pregnancy and might not be able to give you answers at this point. But it would help you to know where he sees himself fitting into the child's life. Does he want to see the child? Or would he prefer to provide financial support but not be there emotionally for his son or daughter? Is he intent on seeing the child two times a week and every other weekend, or would he prefer unlimited access to the child? These are the issues that will be determined in court and spelled out in a legal agreement if you are not able to reach one yourselves.

Are his positions on such issues very far from yours? Clarify in your own mind what you think would be best for the child and decide whether you are willing to compromise.

If your positions are not too far apart but you are still unable to agree, you might consider engaging a mediator. The aim of a mediator, who may be a family law attorney or a child psychologist, is to guide the couple toward a written compromise and agreement. The mediator does not take sides but rather provides insight into similar cases and makes suggestions about the best interest of the child.

A couple with a healthy level of trust may want to hold the agreement between themselves. Others seek a legal agreement documenting the terms that they have settled on. This option involves scheduling a hearing to present the agreement or a written stipulation to a judge who will review the specifics and put it on file as a legal order. I recommend the latter. It helps prevent later litigation should there be estate claims, social-security problems, veteran's dependents benefits, other public claims or a change of heart by the father. Couples who have reached agreement on some issues but not all of them will be able to present those solutions to the court.

If you have not been able to come to terms with your child's father on the issues of child support, custody or visitation schedules, or have not been able to persuade him to meet with you, you will need to enlist the help of a private attorney, the state child-support enforcement agency, the district attorney or an intake officer with the family and domestic-relations court. Occasionally, the delivery of a motion acts as a wake-up call to the father and brings about his cooperation. In other cases, there's a legal battle at virtually every turn.

Legal Representation

If you decide to proceed with legal action, you will first need to decide which route to pursue. Most people choose either a private attorney or a government attorney provided by the state child-support enforcement agency. Self-representation—that is, filing your own papers at the county court and presenting your own case to the judge—is yet another alternative for those who don't have the patience to wait for a hearing date through the child support office or the money to hire an attorney.

Most women base their decision on what they can afford. Private attorneys typically charge $100 to $300 an hour; government agencies provide the same services at virtually no cost. But family law professionals suggest weighing a few other factors besides cost, such as how much money the alleged father makes and how complicated your case might be. For example, a case in which the father is in another state, and thus another legal jurisdiction, could add complications.

But cost is relative to each case, explains Ken Raggio, another former chairman of the family law section of the American Bar Association. "It will cost you very little to have a government lawyer represent you, but as some people say, you get what you pay for. Sometimes they do very well; sometimes they don't. You're one in a million."

GOVERNMENT REPRESENTATION

Anyone, regardless of financial status, can enlist the help of the Child Support Enforcement program (CSE), established by Congress in 1975 under Title IV-D of the Social Security Act, to locate an absent father, establish paternity and/or determine and enforce child support payments. The program, which falls under the auspices of the Department of Health and Human Services, offers legal representation to women through state agencies and county offices.

CSE services are generally free or low-cost, depending on the state of residence. Some states charge application fees of up to $25; other states absorb all or part of the fee or charge the non-custodial parent, in most cases the father.

In 1991, the CSE program was handling 13 million cases nationally. Given that statistic, it's easy to understand why services offered by government agencies will likely be impersonal. In Fairfax County, Virginia, for example, you must speak to an information specialist through a hole in a bulletproof window and are expected to introduce your case history in a large public room that feels much like the waiting room of an airport terminal.

Dealing with the CSE agency can be frustrating. When calling in to check the status of your case, for instance, you will usually encounter many busy signals and long periods on hold. Once you do get through with a phone call, you may be asked by a recorded message to "have your case number ready." That is how the CSE offices will typically identify you. Not surprisingly, the government agencies take longer than private attorneys to close a case.

Government agencies begin legal processes by writing the father a series of letters asking him to come in, sign papers and have blood drawn. "We [private attorneys] just sue," declares Rose, who represented single mothers in an Iowa district attorney's office for several years before going out on her own.

When one of Rose's putative single fathers receives a letter from a district attorney's office, Rose typically responds by writing, "Hell no, he's not the father." She says, "I've actually seen it take as long as three years for the D.A.'s office to return to me again with their challenge." The reason for the delay, Rose points out, is that "the state has a backlog of cases, frequent personnel changes, and the lawyers who represent these women are typically fresh out of law school and usually at the bottom of the pecking order. You can scare them easily."

Dora, the 40-year-old mother of twin girls, began filling out her paperwork for the Virginia child-support enforcement office just before her children were born. Although the Arlington resident was able to give complete information concerning the location of the girls' father, she was not able to get a court hearing until more than a year later. But the checks haven't come yet, and as a result, Dora, who is finishing up a bachelor's degree at American University, was forced to apply for welfare through the Aid to Families of Dependent Children program, as well as government-sponsored child-care. Dora is still awaiting the $900 a month in child support that the court recently awarded her.

Other women, such as Lisa, who filed through the San Francisco district attorney's office, have been thrilled with the government service for obtaining child support.

PRIVATE ATTORNEYS

Not only do private attorneys work faster than government attorneys as a rule, they also give their clients personal attention. When working with a private attorney, you will be greeted cordially by name and probably offered some coffee or juice as you melt into a plush couch within a luxurious reception area. But you also will get a significantly higher bill.

Barber advocates hiring a private attorney in many cases. The benefit of hiring a private attorney, even considering the cost, is that "a private attorney can give personalized attention and be more responsive."

A private attorney will not necessarily get you a higher child-support award or better custody arrangements than a government representative. Both private and government attorneys work within the same state child-support guidelines. In other words, whoever represents you will work with the same charts and present largely the same information to a judge, including salaries, expenses and child-care costs. There is the chance, of course, that a private attorney who has more time to devote to you could present a better argument on more complicated issues or do more research on your case.

If the father of your child is making more than $50,000, Raggio says, there is no question that you should hire a private attorney. You simply cannot afford to have someone make errors. The high volume of cases that government attorneys attempt to take care of increases the chance for mistakes. "You don't want a bank account that holds thousands of dollars to be overlooked," he says.

Carmen spent nearly $8,000 in attorney's fees without even stepping into a courtroom. Although that's a lot of money, she concludes that it was well worth it, because at the time, she needed the support, the hand-holding and the reassurance that a private attorney could provide.

After a few letters were exchanged by the attorneys, Carmen and her son's father were able to agree upon an amount of child support. He suggested a joint checking account in which he would deposit payments to avoid having them lost or delayed in the mail.

Renee, 30, an attorney practicing in New York at the time, was billed nearly $36,000 by the lawyer she hired to help her secure sole custody, her monthly child support and a reasonable visitation schedule for the father. Like doctors who don't perform surgery on themselves or their family, Renee had no intentions of handling her own case.

Pleased with her attorney's services but bent out of shape over the tab, Renee intends to challenge the bill by taking the facts and figures to a legal mediator. You may be able to avoid a situation like this by limiting the work of your lawyer. One common mistake made by clients is to constantly jump on the telephone to call their lawyer for a progress report. You may be surprised to find that a 30-minute phone call can cost you $50.

Instead, search for an attorney who will cap his fees. I was able to negotiate a cap on my legal bill—that is, a dollar amount that my legal fees would not exceed—before I agreed to retain my attorney. And believe me, it paid off. We spent about seven hours in court just waiting for our case to be called before the judge. Had I been paying my attorney by the hour, I would have been frantic.

Additionally, it seems that some attorneys send a great deal of unnecessary correspondence back and forth at the expense of their clients, so I also requested that my attorney limit his correspondence to that which was essential.

Renee's attorney did fight for a little-known benefit that unwed mothers who are awarded child support are entitled to in most states: life insurance on her child's father. Based on the child support, the mother and child have what is called an insurable interest in the life of the father. The policy, which is usually purchased and owned by the mother, is for the financial security of the child in the event that his biological father dies. If the father does not cooperate with forms, signatures and blood tests, the court may order him to comply.

Word of mouth is often one of the best methods of finding a family law attorney. But if you don't have any recommendations from someone who has worked with such an attorney, try calling local single-parenting groups for a reference. Another place to try for references is the county bar association, which usually has a family law committee, as does the state bar association. The American Bar Association has members nationwide. While membership in these organizations does not indicate competence, it does reflect commitment, and each office should be able to provide you with a list of local members.

I came across my attorney, Richard M. Wexell, in *Martindale-Hubbell*, a legal reference book available in both public and law-school libraries. *Martindale-Hubbell* lists attorneys by area and outlines their specialties and major clients. I scanned the pages for one who had been actively involved in the American Bar Association's family law section and/or served on related committees affecting rulings on pressing issues such as blood testing or interstate support enforcement. A few lawyers I had known in other parts of the country who were active on committees of the American Bar Association seemed to be on the cutting edge of various issues.

During your search for an attorney, inquire about average hourly rates and retainer fees on the telephone; ask about free initial consultations. If money is currently a problem, you may be able to find one who will allow you to postpone paying him until the case is closed. In some instances, judges have ordered fathers to pay attorney's fees for the mother.

SELF-REPRESENTATION

The final method of seeking a legal determination of child support, custody or visitation, for those who are either desperate or adventuous enough, is called self-representation. Self-representation means that you file your own paperwork in the courthouse and present your arguments or plea to the judge yourself. Its appeal lies in its relative expediency and affordability.

If you like the idea of self-representation, start with a phone call to your county domestic- and juvenile-relations court to express your interest in representing yourself in court, most likely for a paternity or support case.

To save money, I did a combination of self-representation and representation by a private attorney for my child support and custody cases. I filled out and filed all of the motions and subpoenas to gather financial evidence related to my child support case and brought in an attorney to present the facts and arguments during the hearing. I was only too happy to lay the groundwork and arrange to get the relevant documents into the courthouse, but I did not have the stomach to state my own case to the judge.

The self-representation process began when I met with an intake officer at the county courthouse in Fairfax, Virginia. He helped me fill out paperwork and send out a subpoena to Steve's employer to file pay stubs and records attesting to his salary, tips and commissions. We also requested a copy of his most recent tax returns. Steve was served notice of the hearing within two weeks of my paperwork.

If you plan to present your case yourself, be sure you spend time sitting in on similar hearings so you'll know what to expect during your own. Call your county court to find out which days of the week are reserved for hearings involving child support, custody and visitation. Watching others will both help and strengthen you; the process will not seem so intimidating.

A judge in Virginia's Fairfax County Juvenile and Domestic Relations District Court agrees. "Attend as many hearings as you can in order to prepare," advises Judge Michael Valentine, who says he's seen about 100 people out of 5,000 attempts adequately represent themselves during his 12 years on the bench.

Soon after you file a motion, gather and organize all of your own financial documents that you plan to introduce as evidence, such as pay stubs, child-care receipts, health insurance bills and loan applications. "Make four copies of each piece of evidence," Valentine suggests. You will need to have a copy for your attorney, the child's father and his attorney, the judge and any witnesses during the hearing. "It keeps the trial moving," Valentine notes. "Judges get a little nervous when people walk in with shopping bags filled with papers."

But, Valentine warns, if you appear in court without representation and find that the father of your child has an attorney, "ask the judge for a delay to seek counsel. An experienced lawyer can cite cases and say something like, `Your Honor, this is a Brown vs. Brown case.'" Unless you've been through law school you would probably not know how to respond to such references and legal jargon. Start making calls to find an attorney who can represent you on your next court date or consult with a staffer at the state CSE office.

If your child's father is not represented, you can take a deep breath to help you relax and plan to go ahead as scheduled. Bring a magazine or two to help ease your mind while you wait outside the courtroom, sometimes for hours. Armed with the related facts, figures and documents, you should be able to make your presentation in a respectful, clear and calm fashion. It's perfectly natural, however, to be a bit nervous. Above all, don't allow any anger to surface during the hearing and don't talk out of turn. Keep cool. You can do it!

Financial Matters

While newly pregnant, you may have breezed through the infant section of your local department store and even settled on the nursery decorating scheme. When your child was just a newborn, you might have added his name to a waiting list for a prominent preschool.

Planning for a child, on one hand, can be such a joy, so exciting, in some instances almost dreamlike. It's hard to believe, however, that many parents overlook the most vital planning of all—a short-term health-care plan and a long-term plan that anticipates a future in which you are not here to provide for your child.

As a responsible parent, you must factor in the "What if I'm not around?" scenario and arrange your finances accordingly, taking into consideration life insurance, a will and a trust to work on your child's behalf in your absence. The most important question is, Who will raise your child if you are not there? Naming a guardian and making provisions for your child in the event of your death are part of your most crucial parental responsibilities.

HEALTH INSURANCE BENEFITS

During pregnancy, one of the most pressing financial matters is health insurance. The importance of prenatal care and the guarantee of medical care for both emergencies and the general health of a pregnant woman and her baby cannot be overstated. Yet, not all single mothers have health insurance or maternity benefits. Others who do have insurance make the mistake of not carefully reviewing their policy's for maternity allowances, exclusions, and maximum payouts.

In order to avoid any financial surprises and unnecessary burdens, you should scrutinize the maternity benefits and coverage within your health insurance policy before the birth of your child. Compare the coverage of your health insurance policy with the costs of your local hospital and birthing centers.

Determine exactly which services aren't covered by your insurance policy and which are allowed, and know your deductibles, advises Jerry Rosenbloom, chairman of the life insurance and risk-management department at the University of Pennsylvania's Wharton School in Philadelphia. Call your obstetrician to clarify fees and make note of the average delivery bill, both vaginal and C-section, in the hospital or birthing home in which you plan to deliver.

Rosenbloom also recommends talking to your employer's benefits specialist about disability income and the possibility of borrowing from a savings or retirement plan in an emergency.

The average cost for a normal vaginal delivery in 1991 (the last year for which statistics are available), according to the Health Insurance Association of America, was $4,720. The average monthly payment for an individual's insurance in a conventional group health plan in 1992 was $175.

If you don't have health insurance, "get coverage immediately," states Adriene Berg, a New York tax attorney and financial planner. Look into policies offered through professional groups, associations or organizations of which you are a member. And don't neglect to shop around for the very best rates and policies. "Group rates are not always lower," says James H. Major, agency vice president of the personal insurance division for Metropolitan Life Insurance Co. in New York.

Rebecca, 23, was working at a Club Med resort and living a life of wanderlust when she learned that she was pregnant. As a circus performer and caretaker of the toddlers at the Club Med village in Sandpiper, Florida, Rebecca was given free lodging and meals and $400 a month. Health insurance wasn't included, however. Rebecca returned home to Northern Virginia and opened up the Yellow Pages in search of an insurance company that would offer her coverage. She never found one and instead signed up for Medicaid. "It's free," she explains, "and they're the only ones who would take me." The policy pays for the former nursing student's prenatal visits and will allow her to deliver with a midwife, which gives her more control over the techniques and drugs used during delivery.

If unemployed, consider getting a job, perhaps one for which you are a bit overqualified, with a large company. As an individual purchasing a health insurance policy, you will likely find that most policies have a 12-month waiting period for pre-existing conditions such as pregnancy, says Melanie Marsh, manager of consumer affairs for the Health Insurance Association of America. "But most employers don't have waiting conditions in their health insurance policies," she notes. "The larger the company, the better the benefit package."

When I found out that I was pregnant, I was managing a small magazine and I had no health insurance. I accepted a job with the U.S. government, unaware at the time of the relationship of insurance policies, waiting periods and large companies. I was pleasantly surprised when my supervisor handed me paperwork with nearly 20 insurance policies, some of which offered immediate coverage for prenatal visits and the delivery of my baby.

If you can't afford health insurance, there are a number of public programs that can offer help, specifically with prenatal care. Call your county health office for information.

LIFE INSURANCE

For a relatively small amount of money, you can purchase life insurance, which will enable the dreams you have for your child to live on, regardless of whether you are there to see them materialize.

When I met with my employer's insurance specialist to review my coverage, I learned that my policy provided about $50,000 worth of coverage. But after consulting with a few outside insurance agents, I decided that with the two condominiums that I own and plans for private school for Morgan and outside lessons such as ballet and gymnastics if my daughter wanted, I would need extra coverage. I settled on an additional term life insurance policy for about $20 a month that pays $250,000 in the event of my death.

For about $80 a month, Diane, a mother in Texas, pays for a supplemental term life insurance policy worth nearly half a million dollars. Her sister, son Bobbie's legal guardian, was named beneficiary. Her employer gave her a policy worth about $20,000. "It's worth it; it's peace of mind for me," says Diane, who didn't want her family to have any financial burden for her son.

When purchasing life insurance, decide on both the amount of coverage and on the type of insurance policy—term or whole life, which is sometimes called cash-value insurance. Term insurance is generally preferred by those who have limited funds. It can provide exactly the same dollar value coverage for your child as the more expensive whole-life policies, but it offers you no cash or loan value. Whole-life or cash-value insurance may be considered an investment. Single mothers who are financially secure might want to purchase whole-life insurance as an investment that may provide some tax benefits and funds that may later be borrowed against, generally at low interest rates. The premium on whole-life insurance does not go up as you get older, but the policy's cash value increases annually.

Some financial planners recommend purchasing term insurance no matter what your income level and making your own investments with the money you save by not purchasing a whole-life policy.

When you select an insurance policy or company, it's important to realize that some agents sell only a particular company's line of insurance while others sell for a variety of companies. Don't make the mistake of purchasing a "bargain" policy from an insurer who turns out to be uncooperative or unable to pay its claims.

Today more than ever, warns Major of Metropolitan Life Insurance, it's important to check with a reputable rating service to see how insurance companies and policies measure up. The New York office (212-208-1527) of Standard and Poor's, a ratings and financial information services company, offers free verbal confirmations and ratings for up to five insurance companies based on in-house research. Duff and Phelps produces a similar report, and *Best Insurance Reports* is a publication of the A.M. Best financial rating service.

A WILL

An up-to-date will is another essential for single mothers. The will should name a guardian and a beneficiary and set up a trust. The guardian is someone who would care for your child if you die. The guardian should be a good, nurturing individual, advises Robert B. McCormick, a tax and estate attorney in Fairfax, Virginia.

If you do not name a guardian in your will, the court will assign one—probably the natural father, who has an instant right regardless of whom you name in your will as the guardian and regardless of his prior involvement with the child, McCormick says.

The fact that her son's estranged father could easily gain custody of her son and his estate in the event of her death caused Diane to ask her son's father to relinquish his parental rights. "It would be an emotional disaster for all involved," states Diane, who wants her family to raise her son, Bobbie, if she is not around.

When selecting a guardian, look for someone who is trustworthy and will treat the child as his or her own, suggests McCormick: "People who have children who are grown and out of the home or people who do not have children are ideal."

Renee named her younger sister and her husband as her daughter Melissa's guardian. "They have a daughter, Melanie, who's three and a half," Renee says. "Melanie and Melissa love each other."

You may want to name a guardian for the property of the child, separate and apart from the child as a person, McCormick says. This is normally accomplished by creating a trust. This gives you the power to control the child's assets at least to majority, notes McCormick.

"The trust—property or money left to your child upon your death—is created within your will and is usually funded with a term life insurance policy," McCormick states. Many single mothers make the mistake of listing their child as the beneficiary, he says. But in doing so, they risk enabling the child's father, who may not have even met the child, to control the child's assets and therefore gain access to the child's inheritance. "Some have been known to gain custody of the child's assets, drain the child's inheritance and then put the youth up for adoption. To prevent this, name your estate as the beneficiary."

Also within the will, you need to determine a trustee, someone responsible for protecting your child's assets as well as managing and distributing them in accordance with the terms of the trust. "The trustee should be someone who has a financial background and someone in whom you have absolute confidence," McCormick advises. "It must be someone who is not likely to squander the assets of the trust."

"You could name a bank, your mother or your sister," Berg, the New York tax attorney and financial planner, points out. But some professionals, including McCormick, advise against the choice of a bank as a trustee. "Never name a bank," he warns. "Banks charge high money-management fees and they tend to pay the lowest rate of return. They also tend to be overly conservative." He recommends selecting a paid financial advisor as a trustee.

Some believe it's a mistake to name the same person as both the guardian and the trustee. The benefit of having one individual as the trustee and another as the guardian is that "they can watch each other," notes McCormick.

Drawing up a will can be expensive, and some people consider using fill-in-the-blank wills that are found in books as a way to cut down on the cost. One reference, "Nolo's Simple Wills," by attorney Denis Clifford, includes a will specifically written for a single parent with a minor child. The book claims to feature wills that are legally accepted in every state but Louisiana. But most professionals in the legal field warn against trying to cut corners with a standard will.

When dealing with a significant amount of life insurance and attempting to pass assets to a minor, perhaps your only heir, the cost, usually $250 to $1,000, for a professional to draw up a will is well justified.

Review your will annually and have it revised if you marry, give birth to another child, increase your assets significantly or change your state of residence. When changes occur, execute a new will or add a codicil, a formal document that adds or changes the provisions of the existing will. Distribute copies of your will to a potential guardian, close relatives and perhaps to a member of the clergy.

LAST WISHES

Organize your financial and personal affairs in the form of a letter and place it in an easily accessible place, such as a file cabinet or a dresser drawer. Within your letter or memorandum, which will have no legal validity, write out specific information and figures related to financial obligations, banks, credit cards, outstanding debts, investments such as saving bonds or certificates of deposit and employer savings plans, as well as your social security number and information related to anyone who owes you money. Include copies of appraisals on valuables, such as artworks, jewelry or collectibles, and a legal order for child support if applicable. You may also want to provide a letter to your child detailing the circumstances of his birth, especially in the case of an uninvolved father or one not named in legal documents. If you have a safe deposit box, provide the key, the box number and the address of where it is located.

As to items of sentimental value, indicate to your executor who will retain possession. Of course, it can usually be assumed that it will be your child.

Finally, think long-term. The most important thing to remember, however, is that your decisions should not be quick fixes but rather responsible moves that benefit your child in the long run.

PART 2

❦

SINGLE MOTHERHOOD
by CHOICE

FIVE

The Jolts and Joys of Single
Motherhood by Choice

Mary, an educator, had always wanted to be a mother. But in her late thirties, after years of living in Europe and later pursuing her doctorate, she realized she could no longer put her maternal desires on hold. She moved to Washington, D.C., and made a concerted effort to find a man who would be the father of her children. "I joined tennis and dinner clubs. I met and dated a lot of wonderful men, many who wanted to have children. I always thought that I would meet one to be my husband and have children. But I didn't fall in love." Still, Mary "wanted to love and be loved."

So at age 40, Mary began exploring the two primary ways to form a family without a husband: artificial insemination and adoption. She sat through adoption introductory courses before exploring the cost of artificial insemination and her chances of conception.

It wasn't supposed to be this way. Mary and other single mothers realize that, even before they seriously consider flipping through a sperm bank catalog or taking in a child who may bear no physical resemblance to them. But it appears that these wanna-be moms, also known as single mothers by choice because of their planned pregnancies and deliberate decision to bear or adopt a child without a husband or committed partner, are growing steadily in numbers. In 1991, according to the census bureau, more than 1 million unmarried women gave birth, the highest number ever recorded in the United States. Nearly 200,000 of those births were to women age 30 and older. Accidents do happen, but more often than not, it seems that the older single mothers are educated women who become pregnant by choice rather than by chance.

National figures on adoptions by single mothers are next to impossible to pin down; but in the Washington, D.C., metropolitan area alone, approximately 85 single women per month request information from the Association of Single Adoptive Parents, a regional support and educational group based there.

Several celebrities have expressed support for single mothers by choice. Marianne Williamson, author of *A Return to Love*, is the mother of a child whose father she will not name. And taking this nontraditional route needn't rule out having children in a more traditional fashion later on. At age 35, after the breakup of a relationship with actor Fisher Stevens, movie star Michelle Pfeiffer adopted a biracial baby she named Claudia Rose, before getting married and giving birth to her own biological child.

You, too, may be seriously considering becoming a mother, in spite of the fact that there's no permanent man in your life. If you're like those who go forward, something like the sight of an infant's mobile in a specialty shop, a stroller or the scent of baby lotion probably sends your visions of motherhood spinning. If you ever took the prospect of raising a child for granted in the past, it is not something you do any longer.

Joys of Single Motherhood by Choice

I have no doubt that you could rattle off the blessings of single motherhood by choice if you've given it more than a moment of thought—sweet baby's breath, edible toes, soft lullabies, shopping trips to purchase itsy-bitsy outfits, cuddly toys and bedtime hours filled with children's stories. But the blessings multiply beyond what you can ever imagine. Here are a few you may not have considered.

SPIRITUALLY ALIGNED

Many women describe their quest for motherhood, albeit without a husband, as something spiritual. A woman of Jewish faith who used artificial insemination described her leap into motherhood as one of the most spiritual acts she's ever committed. "A sex act didn't occur," she pointed out, adding, "but I affirmed my own life by saying life is good enough to bring a child into it."

Other women, including an Episcopalian priest, describe their desire to parent as "a calling." And a few, including Mary, who at 41 experienced a flawless pregnancy via artificial insemination, pointed to her son Graham as a reason for her diminished desire for material goods. "I have an old car and it doesn't embarrass me. I don't need to spend $100 on a dress for me right now. I'd rather spend it on him."

THE JOY OF TAKING ACTION

As your internal clock ticks, you may feel especially pressured, even to the point of panic, because of numerous studies showing your limited chances of conception or adoption as a middle-aged woman. As Mary, the woman who played the dating game seriously before opting for donor insemination, pointed out, "The clock ticks; there is just no denying that."

It may be time to act. Schedule a checkup with your gynecologist or mark your calendar for the next meeting of an adoptive parents support group. Perhaps you've been mulling single motherhood over for quite some time and are already familiar with some related facts. As you probably know, both fertility and your chances of adopting a healthy Caucasian infant decline steadily after age 40. Get the ball rolling.

In the United States, in fact, the ideal parents in the eyes of an adoption agency or young birth mother are less than 40 years old. Some agencies will not even place single parents on the rolls. But where there's a will, there's a way. You may just need to think globally, as in international adoptions, or act creatively by spreading the word of your desire to adopt through friends, family and acquaintances.

Luxuriate in the research, planning and preparation for your parenting goal. What fun, what a thrill to secretly scan your insurance carrier's infertility or maternity coverage or your employer's adoption assistance services. What a joy to review your paycheck minus the average cost of a nanny and find out that you may have enough left over to stretch beyond lunches and dinners of Oodles of Noodles.

What can compare with the rush of errands in anticipation of the birth or of meeting your newest family member? Joyce, an adoptive mother, arrived at LaGuardia Airport to meet the plane carrying her two-year-old daughter from India armed with five outfits in various sizes. Joyce also transformed an extra bedroom for her daughter with a playful scheme that included a bright pink bedspread and yellow curtains. About 25 close friends welcomed the child at the airport.

TURNING THE PROCESS INTO A PLEASURE

The tremendous yearning that drives a single mother's decision often turns her pregnancy into sheer joy, labor and all. Such was the case for Linda when she was pregnant with Gretel. "I don't think I stopped smiling, even when my feet and ankles were swollen beyond belief." Jennifer was disappointed when heartburn caused her to be confined to bed for the last two months of her pregnancy and her daughter arrived a month early. "I really felt that the pregnancy ended too soon. I felt cheated because I didn't get to show off my tummy."

For those who adopt, even the frustrations of foreign travel, language barriers and mounds of paperwork and interviews associated with adoption are forgotten once the process nears completion.

WHO NEEDS MEN? THE THRILL OF BEING SELF-SUFFICIENT

Unlike women who harbor resentment after a breakup, single mothers by choice are free to exhilarate in the sheer thrill of pregnancy as they embark on this coveted journey. They are free of expectations tied to another parent. If one happens to come along somewhere down the road, he will be icing on the cake rather than one of the main food groups.

As a single mother, you, like most parents, will probably question your financial security and especially your ability to be the only provider for your child. "You would like to know that you have their college education in the bank," points out one single mother by choice. But it is no surprise to the single mother via insemination or adoption that she must be both a full-time breadwinner, disciplinarian and nurturer, and as a group, single mothers by choice are usually mentally, emotionally and financially prepared to make it on their own. As Jennifer, mother of a child conceived via artificial insemination, concludes, "if you want something badly enough, you'll make it work."

Legal contracts assure these women, as much as possible, that there will be no court battles regarding their children. Many a single mother by choice mentioned that the horror stories of friends in the midst of custody and visitation battles with their child's father made donor insemination or adoption seem blissful.

CREATING A SAFE HAVEN FOR YOU AND YOUR CHILD

The fact that a child is raised by two parents does not necessarily mean he is growing up in a healthy environment.

Plenty of parents fight and argue; many married people have problems with alcohol and abusive behavior of one sort or another. Mary, the educator, says, "Marriage doesn't make a lot of sense to me when I see so many divorces and marriages that are strained."

A single mother, on the other hand, has far more control over her child's environment. In addition to always knowing where the baby's diapers are, she doesn't have to contend with a father who doesn't adhere to her nursery organizing tactics and child-rearing philosophies. Therefore home is more likely to be a peaceful haven, rather than a place for aggression, insults and disagreements between incompatible people. "I don't think Sarah has ever heard me even raise my voice," says Jennifer.

Free from the responsibilities of marriage, a single mother can establish a value system that may be different from the Joneses'. Mary's regime for her son excludes television. "The greatest gift I will give this little boy is time," she says. "Instead of plunking him down in front of the TV set, I hope I'll take him outside or read to him."

HAVING YOUR DREAM COME TRUE

A desire to love someone and have someone love you, a desire to teach and to watch someone grow—parenting without a partner can fulfill these wishes and more.

"I wanted to have someone running to me when she was happy, someone who woke me up screaming 'Mommy' at the top of her lungs. I wanted someone to extend my family and keep me from being alone," explains Bernadette. The adoption of her daughter Louise, from Peru, made that wish come true.

But while it may be tempting to get swept up in the tide of women opting for motherhood outside of marriage, it's unwise to move too fast. If you are seriously considering this option, you need to consider the repercussions.

The Challenges You Will Face

It is hard to overestimate what a tremendous undertaking single parenthood is. Any responsibility, from the cost of annual and seasonal wardrobes complete with rubber boots and mittens to college costs and the logistics of handling sick days and transportation, weighs more heavily on the single parent. The bottom line, notes Jennifer, is that "this little person only has only one person to depend on, and that's me."

Not every woman who fantasizes about parenting alone actually lives out her dream. "About 50 percent of the mothers who contemplate single motherhood in the meetings of the New York–based Single Mothers by Choice organization don't go through with it," says founder and director Jane Mattes. Those who decide against it have many of the same reasons as women who abort accidental pregnancies or place their children through adoption. "They may feel that they don't want to do it alone; it's so hard, and they're frightened," concludes Mattes. They may feel that they cannot surmount the family and social pressure, uncertainty about the child's genes, and the possibility that the child might never have the benefit of a paternal relationship.

MAKING PEACE WITH YOUR DECISION

The first challenge for a single mother by choice is to find peace in her decision to bring a child into this world or to raise a child on her own. "I had to let go of *some* hope [of parenting within a marriage] in order to just move forward in this direction," points out Linda, the mother of 14-month-old Gretel, whom she conceived through artificial insemination.

Many single mothers in accidental pregnancies, while accepting this unconventional introduction to parenthood, hope that their next child will be conceived within a marriage to a man who is elated at the prospect of becoming a parent. For single mothers by choice, however, this route is often viewed as a last call to motherhood.

MONEY MATTERS

Artificial insemination can be an expensive process. Each attempt can run from $200 to $400, depending on a woman's level of fertility and the method of insemination that is used. The price of adoption, which might include the expense of foster care, passport fees, travel money or money for an escort, may total between $7,000 and $12,000 through an agency, which most adopting mothers use. Private adoptions, in which an adoptive mother picks up the tab for a biological mother's medical bills, lodging and in some cases her luxuries, can run higher.

The actual arrival of the child brings another avalanche of expenses, from child care to special equipment, such as a car seat and baby monitor. Of course these expenses are no different from those of any other parents; they just happen to fall solely on one set of shoulders.

Linda, a public relations specialist, confesses to not being budget-minded. She sees it this way: "I made sure that I had a good wad of money in the bank [before taking the leap into single motherhood], because I wouldn't have done this if I could not have given my child a comfortable lifestyle. I still worry about long-term costs, however, such as college and retirement, and I dream every day about winning Publisher's Clearinghouse so that I can stop work and put Gretel in the perfect preschool."

You may wonder whether you have the necessary financial stability to go forward with single parenthood. Many married parents have the same fear. To get a realistic sense of how you would fare with the additional expense of a child, call a few child-care centers and nanny services in your area. To determine where you would stand, subtract from your income the child-care cost—the single greatest expense of raising a young child—plus at least $150 a month for food, diapers and milk. Would you be able to provide a child with all of these things? Would you be able to live comfortably on the income that is left over?

If not, sit down and map out a financial plan to make that goal a realistic possibility. Additional part-time jobs, sending résumés out into the workplace for a career jump and scaling back on material goods can make your dream come true.

FRIENDS AND FAMILY MAY NOT APPROVE

Once you have made up your mind to become a single mother, you will probably share your dream with family members. Most mothers hope that their relatives—the child's grandparents, aunts, uncles and cousins—will play a meaningful role in their child's life. Unfortunately, that doesn't always happen.

As with accidental pregnancies, families and friends of a single mother by choice may be less than supportive. One mother who used artificial insemination sent her brother and sister a note telling them that she was pregnant and asking them to mark their calendar for the arrival of the newest family member. But Jennifer, the 47-year-old free-lance film and television producer in California, never heard from her siblings. And after the written announcement, she began missing out on family gatherings and milestones. For instance, she was not even invited to her nephew's bar mitzvah.

During a chance encounter with her brother at the airport, Jennifer mentioned that her daughter was upstairs in a playroom and that he was welcome to go up and meet her. Before he was able to respond, Jennifer's turn came up at the ticket counter. Seconds later, after her luggage was tagged and her tickets were in order, she redirected her attention toward her brother. He was nowhere in sight.

Her daughter, Holly, has never met her cousins. "It's devastating and it's sad, and I felt those feelings for a long time," explains Jennifer. "But you get to the point—after you've gone through the pregnancy and the birth of your child—where if your family members are negative, you don't want them in your life. You want to be around people who cherish [your child]. I want her to be around people who accept her unconditionally." Other women experience initial disapproval of their single motherhood but find that most relatives come around eventually to accept the child; some even become the child's staunchest role models.

BIRTH PARENTS MAY REMAIN FOREVER A MYSTERY

Society now recognizes the need to know one's heritage. It is a challenge for a single mother who cannot pinpoint a biological father to help her child accept and deal with this reality.

The parentage issue is uniquely difficult for single mothers who adopt children with incomplete birth records or who use sperm banks, which in many cases guarantee the father's right to privacy. In either case, mothers may not be able to offer concrete answers to their child's questions about his parents. (In donor inseminations, fathers are identified by a number rather than a name.)

The issue of whether a donor should be portrayed as a child's father is a controversial one. Many insemination mothers tell their child that he doesn't have a father; others describe the donor simply as someone who helped Mommy give birth.

Many adoptions, especially those done through orphanages, come through without birth records or other information pertaining to parents. Joyce, the 42-year-old adoptive mother of four-year-old Sarah, from India, tried to gather concrete information from the orphanage about her daughter's birth parents but found it impossible. "There was no birth certificate, and many of the orphanages don't keep records," she explains. Joyce was told only that her daughter's birth mother was very young.

The worry about how a child will handle the prospect of not being able to meet a biological parent is a tremendous one for women, and it deters some would-be mothers from going forward with donor inseminations. The following chapters further address this issue and offer concrete advice with regard to rethinking and handling such matters. For most single mothers by choice, motherhood turns out to be all it was cracked up to be. Like all mothers, they are changed forever because of their children.

"Everything in my life is colored by her presence, and everything takes on new meaning," concludes Linda. "Because of her, I care whether the playground has wood chips or pebbles."

"It's a very dependent relationship," says Mary, whose thirst for love was quenched with the birth of her three-month-old son. "I wanted to be part of the world; this is what the world does—raise children."

For those who still have some lingering doubts, the Single Mothers by Choice organization, founded in 1981, has special meetings for "thinkers," a name given to those who are trying to decide, perhaps over a period of a year or two for insemination candidates, whether single motherhood is for them. Membership and the "thinkers" meeting, which is held in New York City, can be expensive.

If you are budget-minded, you might make a few telephone calls to reproductive endocrinologists or adoption agencies in your area instead, merely to schedule a consultation. Most nurses or staff members have reference materials on hand

and at least one person's phone number that they will gladly pass along to you as an information source.

For those leaning toward adoption, Families Adopting Children Everywhere (FACE) offers a six-week introductory course to the process. You can request information by calling (410) 488-2656.

If you prefer to keep your anonymity or would like to read more on the subject, you can find newspaper and magazine articles that were written about the subject of single motherhood by choice in the *Readers' Guide to Periodicals*, a reference found in most public libraries.

Six

Test-Tube and Donor Daddies

It first flickers into a single woman's consciousness at around age 32. By the time she's 35 or 40, an occasional worry has become a nagging anxiousness, and in another four or five years it may be an almost overwhelming yearning. The biological clock is winding down; it's the last call for a healthy body to conceive before the onset of menopause.

Initially, the call isn't taken seriously. That day may come only after the realization that Prince Charming isn't coming to your rescue—or, if he is coming, he may not be in time for you to give him a child. Many women link the realization to a rite of passage, such as a fortieth birthday or the witnessing of someone else's wedding.

In mourning the loss of the dream of a traditional family, some women wonder if perhaps they could have been a little more tolerant of a past beau's pranks or another one's lack of drive. You may wonder if you've been too judgmental. One woman, Linda, had those same pangs of guilt and foolishness after her own father informed her that she had been "too picky." "I looked back and I thought, I could have made that relationship work," confided Linda. But her feelings changed after she bore a child via artificial insemination without having to settle for a man who wasn't Mr. Right. Now, Linda knows that she made the right decisions all along.

Increasingly, single women who don't have a steady are turning to artificial insemination as a way to experience motherhood. Its appeal lies in the fact that it is relatively safe, simple and affordable. The process typically involves monitoring your temperature or urine to determine ovulation, and recruiting a donor or purchasing prize breeder sperm from a sperm bank after scrutinizing a donor's physical characteristics, hobbies and family health history.

Jennifer, who became pregnant via artificial insemination, came to view the issues of marriage and motherhood separately as her child-bearing years dwindled. She vividly recalls the moment she felt the desire to parent most intensely, at age 40, while sitting in her car gazing out over a parking lot.

Watching an older woman and wondering what her life was like, Jennifer, an independent producer of television shows and films, began visualizing what her own life would be like 10 years down the road. "Fifty alone without a husband would have been OK; 50 alone without a child was not. I think I would have been a very bitter woman for the rest of my life. I would have been angry that just because I never had a husband, I never had a child."

And while Jennifer, who is now the mother of 22-month-old Holly, and others like her can't guarantee a father for their child, they can increase his or her chances of some enviable attributes in life with an ideal selection of smarts, stature and genes.

What we don't know for certain, however, is how this new breed of children, born to single mothers via donor insemination, will react to having access to a donor's vital statistics but not necessarily his name and phone number. In this chapter, we'll walk you through your decisions with the child's best interest in mind, an interest that has been overlooked in far too many donor inseminations in the past.

Women who pursue donor insemination must confront challenges that may include societal and family opposition, the difficulty of explaining to a child his unique conception and problems related to raising a child without access to the father's identity.

Statistics on artificial inseminations are sketchy; the last official tally in 1986 found that 197,000 births were assisted by artificial insemination that year. The option is truly in the air these days, as evidenced by the new Jaglom film *Baby Fever*. Estimates indicate that around 1 million donor-conceived people are alive today, many of whom were born to single women. An estimated 25 percent of the women seeking donor insemination from the California Cryobank in Los Angeles are single, according to spokeswoman Ronda Wilkin.

If the idea of a child that is 100 percent yours seems appealing, you'll want to further explore the logistics, the feelings and the issues involved in donor insemination for the single woman. Such issues, from the search for paternal genes to the signing of legal contracts, are all touched upon in this chapter. We'll also look ahead to such long-term issues as telling your child about his conception and preparing for his reaction.

The Lure of Artificial Insemination

Jacqueline, age 38, a free-lance book editor and writer in California, has toyed with the notion of pursuing artificial insemination for years. "I like me and I like my genes," she declares cheerfully. "I'm a sensitive, caring person, and I know I would be that type of mother, whether married or not. I want my child to have those characteristics."

In deciding between artificial insemination and adoption, Jacqueline found great reassurance in knowing she would be familiar with at least half of the gene pool from which her baby would draw his or her physical, mental and character traits. Other women choose artificial insemination over adoption because of their desire to experience pregnancy, labor and childbirth. "She is scared, scared to run out of time," wails Bonnie Raitt in one country-flavored ballad. Many single women, maybe even you, feel the same way. As Jacqueline succinctly puts it, "I want to have a child from my own body." And it's not a feeling for which you need be ashamed.

San Francisco reproductive endocrinologist Robert Nachtigall explains why. Be it an occasional pang or a very strong desire, Mother Nature doesn't discriminate between the married and unmarried. "Because women have a monthly hormonal cycle, they can't escape the fact that their bodies are telling them to do something," Nachtigall told *Time* magazine. "The biological drive to reproduce may be stronger than the cultural yearning to get married." As for the unmarried woman who nevertheless gives in to the mothering urge, Nachtigall argued that "while such a choice is unconventional, it is also quite natural."

As Mary, 42, sat in a crowded room full of couples listening to a presentation about adoption, she realized that many of those present were experiencing infertility problems. "It really touched me, because I sat there thinking, `I'm not infertile.'" The 42-year-old educator is now the mother of a three-month-old son conceived via artificial insemination.

The procedure cost Mary only $1,500, a lot less than the $5,000 she discovered she would have to pay for an adoption. [Mary's health insurance covered the cost of certain medications related to the procedure, such as the Chlomid and Perginol she took to get her hormones up to snuff. She picked up the tab for the actual insemination.] Like Mary, you may find that, depending on your ability to conceive and your insurance policy, artificial insemination is less expensive and faster than an adoption.

It was natural for Lauren, an Episcopal priest in her late thirties working for a nonprofit organization, to consider adoption when she began researching possible routes to single motherhood. "The idea of providing a home for a poor, starving orphan sounds appealing," she says, "but there are more people wanting to provide homes than there are poor, starving orphans. It was not an option that was open to me, and it isn't to most people, unless they are in a picture-perfect situation."

Lauren found that most birth mothers and domestic agencies consider the ideal adoptive parent to be under 40 years old, a homeowner and in a position to hire a nanny or be a stay-at-home parent. Some adoption agencies will not even allow a person to join the rolls of prospective parents unless he or she has remained at home for the past year. Few can afford that luxury. "I had to work," Lauren says, "and I couldn't be home with a child who needed perpetual care, and I was not in a position to take an older child." An overseas adoption would have cost her between $8,000 and $12,000 in air fares and legal fees, which she didn't have. Before pursuing artificial insemination and eventually landing a donor she recruited herself, the resourceful priest concluded, "It made no sense for me to buy a baby when I could have one of my own."

Some women grapple with the idea of getting pregnant through what I call a donor-in-the-dark route to motherhood. The thought of a sexual relationship with an unsuspecting partner did cross Mary's mind, but it was just in passing. "I did not want to have a child without the consent of another individual," she says. In contrast to a donor in the dark, artificial insemination is a more respectable method of single motherhood. It's on the level. Seeking motherhood by using a man without his knowledge is deceptive and dishonest.

A CONTROVERSIAL ROUTE

A sense of obligation to her child, as well as fear of what spiritual elders and family members might think, can give a woman pause when considering artificial means of conception.

Kristi Hamrick, spokeswoman for the Family Research Council in Washington, D.C., speaks for many when she expresses her preference for single women to "pour out their energy on the children currently out in the world who need mothering." This school of thought favors single women becoming adoptive or foster mothers as well as "big sisters" who devote time to children within dysfunctional families.

She believes that single women who seek motherhood via artificial insemination are approaching parenthood as a what-is-best-for-me issue, rather than considering what is best for the child. She criticizes a line of thinking that in her view goes something like this: "I'm going to choose the best I.Q., try to determine how tall my child will be, what possible skills he will have and maybe even if it will be a him or a her. I'm going to have a designer baby on my terms."

We're forgetting that children are both a gift and a privilege but not a right. It's not enough to say, "What would I want in my life?" as opposed to "What could I do for a child long-term?"

Others, like Hilary Hanafin, chief psychologist at the Center for Surrogate Parenting in Beverly Hills, see the issue as a difficult one to evaluate. "We're looking at a philosophical argument in terms of whose needs are being met and whether these children would be better not existing, as opposed to not having a father figure."

"It is very clear from all of the research that children do best in a two-parent family," points out Hamrick. "A father and a mother bring unique and different skills to the parent-child relationship. Mothers are vital in the early years to provide a foundation and a sense of self-esteem," she says. "A father is the `go for it' person." Hamrick cited studies revealing that children who do not have contact with their father find it harder to make friends, harder to socialize and harder to do well in school.

Genetic engineering is a big moral issue these days. Tampering with the natural order of the birth process is viewed as sinful by some religious groups.

It is a natural concern for those of us with religious beliefs to explore how insemination fits into our spiritual upbringing. But most women have found their church supported their pregnancy. Soon after Lauren gave birth to Eve with the help of a donor whom she knew, she was thrown a baby shower by her parish.

Mary, the educator, solicited the support of her priest before going ahead with single motherhood via insemination. She was worried about the route to motherhood because in her religion, she was skipping a sacrament. Matrimony traditionally preceded childbirth. But the clergyman blessed his parishioner's desire, concluding: "God wants you to enjoy your life, and that includes love. The way in which you find love doesn't really matter."

Additional support for artificial insemination comes from some surprising sources. Planned Parenthood, although it doesn't have a formal position on the issue of single mothers and artificial insemination, is "in favor of anything that increases a woman's reproductive choices," says spokesman Michael Policar. The organization believes that "the potential mother is in the best position to make that choice."

PRACTICALLY SPEAKING: IT'S NOT QUITE ORGASMIC

Whether to go forward with artificial insemination is a personal decision that often takes a great deal of time. You don't have to say yes yet. But if you are intrigued enough by the option to explore its ramifications, you can start by making an appointment with a physician. Your physician will perform an evaluation which will include a pelvic exam and some tests for sexually transmitted diseases. One of the most important findings will be whether your hormones are up to speed in terms of conception or in need of some type of supplement.

The results will also give you a more realistic sense of the expense of this route. For women whose bodies need a little help getting pregnant, the fertility drugs and more complicated inseminations often escalate the cost.

Jennifer was 42 when she had the big "B" (baby) talk with her ob-gyn. The two concluded that they would try to get her pregnant in the "most cost and time-efficient manner." Age alone showed that the odds were against the California television producer. Her chances of success were a mere 7 to 12 percent.

"I need one month of your life," the doctor told Jennifer, who was then put through a myriad of tests to check her cycle, her tubes, her mucus and, finally, the strength of her uterus. Jennifer took the gamble and is now the proud mother of two-year-old Holly.

After your physical, make an appointment for a consultation with a full-service sperm bank, a reproductive endocrinologist or an ob-gyn to discuss the procedure in detail. Many of these establishments, which are often listed in the Yellow Pages under "Infertility" or "Physicians," have social workers on hand who will present the issues surrounding artificial insemination and help determine if you are truly ready to proceed.

"A lot of women think of holding a baby in their arms, but they don't exactly have a game plan. They're not thinking of a long-term future with a child," notes Carolin Ringwall, a nurse in the reproductive endocrinology department at Columbia Hospital for Women in Washington, D.C.

During initial consultations with single women, clinical psychologist Elaine R. Gordon, Ph.D., explores the psychological issues and any possible reservations about artificial insemination and makes sure that her patients don't harbor any humiliation with regard to this parenting option. "Sometimes you uncover some inadequacy and shame felt by women who couldn't find a partner," she notes. For the health and well-being of the family, Gordon, who is in private practice and on the staff of Santa Monica Hospital in Los Angeles, also stresses to each mother the importance of feeling completely comfortable with what she is about to do.

During a consultation, a potential mother can see the equipment for the procedure and learn about the two types of inseminations: intra-cervical (ICI) and intrauterine (IUI). Depending on the regularity of your menstrual cycle, you will most likely be inseminated once or twice each month. The inseminations are timed to occur around ovulation.

Most women under 30 with regular menstrual cycles have intra-cervical inseminations because they are fertile and it is quite easy for them to conceive with this method of insemination. At $150 for the specimen, plus $85 for the intracervical insemination at the Columbia Hospital for Women in Washington, D.C., it's effective for them and less expensive than intrauterine. Nurses can generally administer intracervical inseminations, in which the semen is injected into the cervical opening through a plastic tube.

The other method, intrauterine, involves inserting a speculum containing a specially washed specimen, cleaned for the removal of non-sperm cellular matter that can cause infection, and injecting the sperm directly into the uterine cavity. A doctor must perform the intrauterine inseminations, which run $200 for a specimen and $175 for the actual insemination at Columbia. These inseminations are typically used for women of any age who have fertility problems. A plastic-coated sponge or cap may be placed in the vagina before the speculum is removed. The cap keeps the sperm up near the cervix; it can be removed about five hours after the insemination.

With either type of insemination, your road to pregnancy will involve microscopes and slides, bright lights, sperm counts and catheters. Forget romance; you're after results. Most women get excited while watching their frozen sperm specimens thaw before the insemination, and some of their doctors even encourage their participation in preparation for the insemination by allowing them to look at the sperm through the microscope or handle the specimen.

Asked what she thought about during her insemination, which took just minutes, Sabrina, a Washington journalist, told me, "Oh, I don't know. Close your eyes and think of paradise."

Of the actual process, "It's not too much different from a Pap smear," says Jennifer. "My doctor told me a lot of funny sperm jokes. It is possible," she noted, "to sit there on the table and dwell on the reality that, yes, your body has been invaded and you don't know whom the semen is from; but then the emotional side of you and the excitement take over."

A few women complain of minor cramps after their inseminations, usually an indication that too much sperm was injected or that it wasn't properly processed to remove non-sperm cellular matter. Barbara Raboy, executive director of the Sperm Bank of California in Oakland, has heard women who have never had sex with a man before or who have never had sperm in their bodies describe a burning or an itching sensation when inseminated.

One frustrating reality of artificial insemination is that, as in love-making, conception doesn't always occur. Factors such as a patient's age, fertility history, the number of inseminations per cycle, the method of insemination timing used and whether hormonal stimulations and drugs were used can all influence the outcome.

When it came time for her fifth donor insemination, one mother-to-be, Linda, was so emotionally drained and frustrated after the process of carefully selecting her four previous donor choices that she left the selection of the new donor up to her nurse. "It was expensive, I was getting impatient, and it was such a roller-coaster of emotions. At that point, I needed someone to take me by the hand."

Linda had been choosing tall, thin Nordic men from the sperm bank's catalog, and she would probably never have selected the five-foot-nine donor with curly red hair. But based on his track record, her nurse thought he was a good prospect. Linda recalls vividly what happened next. "When the sperm is defrosted, you're considered lucky if you get a sperm-count rating of three. His was a four-plus! We were all singing; we were just dancing around the room, because we knew this was it!"

After the insemination and a 10-minute rest, Linda began the most difficult part of the process: waiting. It's generally two weeks before a pregnancy test can be considered valid. If you're like most, you won't be able to resist the temptation to take your own pregnancy test at home. When Linda's nurse called to congratulate her and tell her that her pregnancy had begun, she was thrilled but not at all surprised.

In Search of Genes: The Sperm-Bank Route

Perhaps the most important decision a single woman will make with regard to insemination is whether the donor she selects will be anonymous or someone whom her child can one day identify and perhaps even meet. This decision will limit your choice of banks, since most of them offer anonymous donors. However, you should not make this decision in haste.

Jennifer chose an anonymous donor from a bank that was certified by the American Tissue Association. Her daughter, Holly, will not have the legal option of finding her donor father, nor he of finding her. Jennifer links her choice of an anonymous donor over an identifiable one to her empathy for adopted children who have unearthed parents who don't care to have relationships. She decided on an anonymous donor in order to save her daughter from any possible rejection.

"I don't know if she'll want to know who her donor father is. It's not quite like the immaculate conception, but I'm hoping that because we look so much alike Holly won't really think about what the other person looks like. " Jennifer believes rejection can be more agonizing than not knowing.

Historically, anonymous donors have been preferred, according to Hanafin, the chief psychologist at the Center for Surrogate Parenting in Beverly Hills. "The women felt that if they loved their child enough, he or she would easily resolve the fact that there was purposefully a non-father figure."

When pursuing artificial insemination through a bank and with an anonymous donor, a potential mother will be asked to sign a contract in which she agrees that she will not now, or at any time, require or expect the bank to obtain or divulge the name of the donor or any other identifying information. A donor signs a similar contract saying that he will not attempt to seek parents or offspring.

But in recognition that the agreement was made with the mother and the donor but not with the child, most banks strive to maintain accurate records and to track donors if the need to break anonymity arises because of medical concerns, or should a court one day grant donor-insemination children the same rights as those in adoptions.

Although the California Cryobank does not currently offer an identity release option because it believes that neither a mother nor a donor can determine during insemination how he or she will feel 18 or 30 years down the road if the child expresses an interest in locating the donor, it does offer an "openness program."

The bank recognizes that the child may have an interest in seeking out his donor. But its policy is not to break the donor contract except by mutual consent. If the donor of a child who is at least 18 years old can be located and is willing to have his identity disclosed, the bank will comply with the child's request. If not, the information will not be released.

In the past five years, however, Hanafin has noticed two changes in the habits of women buying sperm. "They have decided to become better consumers. Women want more information than the banks provide. They're less satisfied with the fact that the bank is in control of the information. They are taking the stance of why would you let anybody but yourself be in control of such information?"

Second, Hanafin has observed that more women are seeing that it may be an issue for the child that he was purposefully conceived without legal access to identifying information about his donor father, such as his name and social security number. "We have seen some grown donor children grieve and be angry with their mother over this fact," warns Hanafin.

Only a few banks currently offer donors who are willing to be identified. Among those are the Sperm Bank of California in Oakland and the Pacific Women's Health and Reproductive Services in San Francisco.

Today, according to Raboy, the executive director of the Sperm Bank in Oakland, nearly all single women who purchase specimens from the facility select donors signed up under the identity-release option. Interestingly enough, the values of the donors are changing as well, she notes. A third of her available donors are willing to release their identities. Over the past six months, though, nearly half of her donor applicants in the midst of screening have granted such permission.

The Sperm Bank of California, like most banks that offer an identity-release option, keeps the donor's name, place of birth, permanent address, phone number and social security number on file and will furnish the donor's offspring with that information after the child reaches age 18. The bank does not guarantee, however, that the information it has on file will be current. It will be the offspring's responsibility to locate his donor father, if he desires. But armed with the donor father's full name and social security number, he should find the task to be relatively simple.

As Raboy points out, "We are in the business of getting people pregnant. And for years and decades, banks have been doing it without truly considering what's in the best interest of the child. This is a movement for the rights of the children."

Had identity release been an option 30 years ago, at least one donor child might have been less obsessed with his origins. In an appearance on NBC's *Now*, Greg Wiatt told about his torment related to his conception via donor insemination. He even broke the law to get some answers.

Determined to find out exactly where he came from and why his donor father had sold his sperm, the young man picked the lock of the sperm bank and went through several thousand records in search of the file that held his birth record. In the process, Wiatt, then 28, discovered that four half-sisters lived in his neighborhood—including one who had sat in front of him in one of his high school classes and whom he had almost dated.

Another donor child on the television program, Melody Leslie, described searching through yearbooks for her biological father, , comparing features of medical students to her own and thinking, "Now, this guy's very handsome. It would be nice to be related to him. It might make sense to put him on the list." In spite of the fact that Melody's chances of finding her biological father are slim, she feels compelled to keep trying. Her anguish is apparent. "I feel like I'm hybrid. If there's anything that I find maddening about the situation, it's the idea that intelligent, really highly educated people would have fooled themselves with the wishful thinking that it wouldn't matter, that it would be inconsequential to me about my biological and genealogical background."

SPERM YOU CAN BANK ON

Before you select a bank, you will want to explore its safety practices and accreditation. While sperm banks are essentially self-regulating, the American Tissue Association has accredited six of them, and the organization encourages women to use them. In the past 10 years, the screening processes have become more rigid. One reason is that there are cases in which the HIV-virus has been transferred through donor insemination. Go with one of the six accredited banks.

The California Cryobank in Los Angeles is not only accredited but also one of the largest full-service sperm banks in the country. Only 8 percent of the men who apply to its donor program are accepted; their sperm count must be in the top 5 percent of all men in terms of fertility. If the initial health report is good, the sperm is frozen and quarantined for at least six months while it is tested twice for hepatitis B, CMV, chlamydia, gonorrhea, SMA 12 (SGPT), HTLV-1, color blindness, cystic fibrosis, syphilis, blood type, HIV and hepatitis C, and once for CBC, Tay Sachs and sickle-cell anemia. Most banks keep recently donated sperm quarantined while fresh samples of the donor's blood are tested for HIV. Only after the later blood tests will the bank offer the donor's sperm to customers.

Raboy explained that the screening process in most banks in-volves a combination of fill-in-the-blanks forms and blood and urine tests. "Much of the information, such as drinking habits, is subjective," says Raboy. "But we do drug testing of urine. And if someone is abusing drugs or alcohol, we should be able to see it in those tests if his body was influenced by drugs. In some cases, he may be ruled out because of a lower sperm count."

Some women order sperm from a bank located across the country so that they won't be wondering about every man on the street who fits their donor's description. Others like the fact that a nearby bank is accredited by the American Tissue Association or has been referred to them by their doctor.

When ordered, frozen sperm can be shipped in liquid nitrogen tanks directly to your doctor. If it's purchased at a local bank, you can pick up the sperm specimen yourself in similar tanks and packaging. Some take it directly to the doctor's office. Others, such as Sabrina, leave it in the back of the car and drive around with it for days.

Although it was destined for her doctor's office, Jennifer, the woman who had the 7- to 12-percent chance to conceive, set her sperm in the front seat next to her, turned on the radio and took the scenic route. "Somehow, I thought it would make a difference, even though I knew it was ridiculous to think that I could have a relationship with that sperm."

But according to Ringwall, the nurse at George Washington University Hospital for Women, "Most choose to purchase sperm from faraway locations. Psychologically, it's better to be separated by distance."

PICKING A DONOR

You've probably used catalogs to order pantyhose, botanical prints, maybe even a tube of sex gel. But who would have thought that the donor father of your child might come from such a book, a book of men—hundreds of them. With so many men to choose from, full heads of hair, statures of six feet and more and good eyesight are among the top factors preferred by women as they scan sperm-bank catalogs and profiles in search of genes.

Women can request brief profiles for about $10 and longer ones for about $25, which touch on donor hobbies and athletic abilities as well as drug and alcohol use and sexual habits. There's even a direct question about why the donor decided to sign up for this rigorous program.

Donors at the California Cryobank are between ages 19 and 34, as are most from other banks. Many are graduate or medical students. Sperm banks often recruit students from selected universities through notices in their campus newspapers.

After scanning a few donor profiles and essay questions profiling donors' personal information, you will realize that virtually all donors participate in the insemination program for the money. They earn between $35 and $50 per visit.

Donor No. 2037 of the California Cryobank, in response to the question of why he wanted to be a donor, wrote, "I have no ethical or moral dilemmas with the procedure. The cash is handy." He described his hobbies, interests and talents as "sports and women." The one message he wanted to pass along to the recipient of his semen was "work hard and enjoy your life."

With so much known about these donors, it's even possible to do professional genetic counseling. As Jennifer noticed, "I have more information about my donor than about any man I've ever had relations with."

For Jennifer, the thought of selecting a biological father from a couple of hundred profiles was emotionally overwhelming. When the plain envelope bearing the list arrived in the mail, she retreated into the bathroom and took a seat. "I saw the list and freaked out. The tears started flowing. `Oh my God,' I thought. `*This* is how I'm going to pick the father of my child.'"

Jennifer first reduced her list from 215 to 36 donors after she asked the bank to identify only the Jewish men. Then, when three good friends volunteered to help weed out some more, Jennifer took advantage of the offer and formed a selection committee. The support of the committee, which consisted of a doctor and a married couple, gave Jennifer the strength she needed: "I didn't feel so alone, and I really valued the input of the men."

The committee explored everything. The doctor zeroed in on such things such as headaches and what a potential donor's grandparents had died of. The second panel member, a mother, paid close attention to headaches, allergies and asthma, each of which nixed a donor. Her husband looked for donors who played sports.

Jennifer scrutinized the donors' handwriting. "Some had very tiny handwriting, and you felt like they were very rigid and very precise; others had a more free-flowing style and seemed more easy-going."

Down from 36 to 12, to 6, to 2. In spite of all their valued advice, the selection committee wasn't let in on the final donor decision. Jennifer kept that information to herself. "This was a personal decision and a private matter," she whispers. "The final decision was mine. I wanted to have one thing that I knew and they didn't." Jennifer ended up consulting with her donor counselor to get insight into her donor's physical appearance. Based on her counselor's insight into the two donors, she ended up going with the one she felt was her type.

Each woman's set of criteria for pinpointing her ideal donor is different. For some, it's the physical package—e.g., blue eyes like their own are a must. For others, it's an ethnic background or a particular career interest that makes them feel as if he's a decent guy, and that may be important to them.

But regardless of what factors you're trying to evaluate, you won't be allowed to catch a glimpse or even a snapshot of him; your decision will be based largely on a written description of facts and figures. Some women consult with sperm bank staffers and counselors who see the donors firsthand. So while you won't be allowed to lay eyes on the men from which you're choosing, that doesn't mean impressions related to physical looks can't be part of the process.

In order to make her final selection, Jennifer presented 10 pictures of men to whom she was physically attracted to her donor-matching counselor. Some of the images had been clipped from magazines; one was a snapshot of a co-worker at an office party. She asked the counselor to compare those with the physical types of the two donors she was considering. The counselor knew both donors and pinpointed one of them as "definitely" her type. To Jennifer, "that was important."

After finding a few donors with clean bills of health and with no sign of birth defects, Mary, an educator, chose one who had graduated from the University of Virginia and worked as a fund-raiser. "He struck me as someone who was potentially bright. Perhaps he had a different type of testosterone—he wasn't a marine; he wasn't a football player. He struck me as someone who had a social disposition."

Blond hair and blue eyes were essential to Sabrina when she scanned the sperm bank catalogs for a donor. In fact, many of the physical attributes of the man she selected, a 28-year-old internist with fair skin and a European background, matched hers. That was part of the plan.

"I wanted the best possible choice of a donor," declares Sabrina. And while good health and intelligence were considered basic, "the most important thing was that he be as physically like me as possible." Sabrina didn't want her son "to be totally different from other relatives. I wanted to give him as many family links as possible."

Like Sabrina, Linda checked the sheets looking first for physical attributes, but hers were of a different nature. "I looked for somebody tall and thin because I'm *not*," says Linda, who stands about five-feet-five. "I tried to give my child attributes that I could not pass along."

At the California Cryobank in Los Angeles, there is a counselor on staff who specializes in photo matching. "We get pictures from mothers who might want the shape of their eyes matched to those of a donor. We also have women who send in pictures of their fathers or brothers," says spokeswoman Ronda Wilkin.

Other women clip out magazine pictures of "dream men"—male models and attractive actors such as Tom Cruise, Robert Redford and Denzel Washington, notes Wilkin. "We've even had pictures of Fabio. Whoever's hip at the time."

Wilkin hasn't noticed any universal requests concerning donor attributes, but she did observe that women can't resist the temptation to select what appears to them to be, at least on paper, "the perfect man."

And who can help but wonder about the physical attractiveness of a bank's donors? Wilkin offers the curious this insight: "Most are really nice guys, but I don't have any that you would really die over."

WHAT DOES HE REALLY LOOK LIKE?

Women considering donor insemination may have heard alarming stories such as the Cecil B. Jacobsen case in Alexandria, Virginia, involving the fertility doctor with the startling looks, who may have fathered as many as 70 children using his own sperm while telling women they were using that of a legitimate donor.

Candace Turner, the 45-year-old founder of Donors Offspring, believes that she, too, resulted from the sperm of the doctor her mother consulted, rather than the Englishman her mother was led to believe was the donor. Turner recalls a nurse on *Geraldo* hidden behind a screen who told of "a mean and nasty woman who came in to purchase sperm and was sold the ugliest man's sperm that they could find, rather than from the donor she had selected on the profile."

Turner and her organization, based in Sarcoxie, Missouri, stand for openness in donor inseminations. She would like offspring to have as much paternal information as possible and for mothers to be able to use video profiles of donors. "If I had a completed donor insemination package of my father with a videotape showing how he walks down the road, how he holds a cigarette, and if my mother had had some counseling as to how to treat the subject of my conception, I wouldn't have had these painful, stressful times. I would have had more of a sense of completion."

A DONOR TALKS

Northern European, six feet tall, 180 pounds. Brown hair, brown eyes, student of international affairs. Hobbies: sports and reading.

As a junior in college, Jack, whose donor profile matched the description above, was a handsome but prematurely bald student. He was drawn to the following notice run by a Fairfax, Virginia, sperm bank in his college newspaper. "It was a real juicy ad," Jack recalls. "It said exactly what I would fall for at the time: It alluded to easy money and quick cash." Jack told me that he saw the extra money as a way to help him entertain his girlfriend, who was two years his senior and already in the work force.

He had no history of medical problems, and when he applied for the donor program, he took the 20-odd pages of the health questionnaire home and filled it out to the best of his knowledge. Donors do not get any additional money if they are selected, so it isn't financially profitable for them to paint a perfect profile.

But Jack was afraid that complete honesty about some of his habits might ban him from acceptance into the donor program. So when it came to questions related to his drug and alcohol habits, Jack lied. For alcohol use, Jack filled in one drink a week; he also said that he had no history of drug abuse. The truth is, Jack had been an occasional user of marijuana, and at the time of his donations he drank a lot. "I used to booze it up all the time. I drank about two to three six-packs a week.

"I did it strictly for the money," states Jack, now 27 and working for a retail establishment. He made close to $1,000 from the donor program. Jack envisions a family rather than a single woman using his sperm. He hasn't asked and does not care to know right now whether he has any offspring.

Jack's contract guaranteed his anonymity, and when I asked if he would be willing to meet with any of his offspring if they requested to do so, Jack got somewhat defensive and then waffled. "I would want to know more about this person and why he wanted to meet me. I was there for the bucks, rather than for my sense of being a father... I really hope that doesn't happen."

Personally Recruited Donors

Because of the concern for their adopted child's interest in his genetic heritage, more women are finding their own donors. Specimens from these men, called designated donors, can be put through the same tests as those from men recruited by sperm banks.

"It's more work," says Elaine Gordon, a clinical psychologist in private practice and on the staff of Santa Monica Hospital, who refers to such arrangements as open donations. "And it can be more expensive. But you get to meet them [potential donors] and know who they are."

You can start your own bank using men you know or those you've recruited, perhaps through advertising.

Regardless of what type of donor you use, you will want to enlist the screening services of a bank. In most states, the law requires that sperm be held for six months and checked for various diseases.

After researching sperm banks and artificial insemination, Lauren concluded that the services of banks and doctors were too expensive and unnecessary, so she took a more active approach of hand-picking her donors, forsaking all doctors and screening procedures, and inseminating herself at home.

Most banks and reproductive endocrinologists do not recommend home inseminations or the use of fresh sperm, which was standard practice in banks in the past. Frozen sperm is today's norm. In fact, in some states, the use of fresh sperm for inseminations is against the law.

Fresh sperm and home inseminations can be a risky route to motherhood. One of Lauren's donors died of AIDS a year after her inseminations, although she says he tested negative for the HIV virus. She and her child have since tested negative for the virus.

But her search for a donor was an interesting one. "I started off with romantic notions of getting someone handsome, brilliant and everything else," says the Episcopalian priest. She began talking to relatives of good friends. At first, she thought that someone who lived far away would be ideal but quickly learned that "working with someone far, far away when you ovulate was difficult and had practical limitations." Eventually, she talked to all the men she knew.

Lauren made it clear to potential donors that this would be her child and no one else's. After watching a best friend go through legal hassles with her ex-husband, she stressed to her potential donors that she was in search of "a donor and not a father" for her child. She went on to package the request as a favor, "a mere donation of a waste product, a favor to a friend that had no further implications."

"I got turned down a lot," explains Lauren, who claims she got bolder as she went along. Some men had children of their own and felt that donating to Lauren would be unfair to them; others had wives and girlfriends who objected. A few men thought it would just make them nuts to do this.

Along the way, Lauren ruled out those with health problems and extreme physical characteristics, such as a very short stature or an unusually large nose. Lauren looked for men who were "kind of average in appearance, because you never know who your child is going to look like."

The ultimate plan involved three donors, whom Lauren eventually secured. She describes them as men who were peripheral in her life and whom she thought a great deal of, although she was not particularly close to any of them.

After an evening of dinner and conversation at Lauren's house, one of the gentlemen in question retired to the upstairs bathroom, where he found a little jar provided for him. The routine was repeated with the other two donors on consecutive evenings. "Afterward, they came down and we hugged."

After each man left, Lauren ran up to the bedroom and inseminated herself with fresh sperm. She used a syringe that she had purchased from a drug store, with the needle removed. "It was very simple, painless and personal." She does not know which man is her seven-year-old daughter's father, and they do not know if her child is theirs or not. "Even if I had a hunch, do you think I would admit it?" says Lauren. When Eve was born, the donors all sent christening gifts.

DONORS IN THE DARK

Some women initiate sexual relations with the sole intention of getting pregnant—sometimes with men they've been dating and sometimes with men they've known only a few hours. Their aim is not to secure a man but to have a child. As mentioned earlier, I call these men donors in the dark.

I have never had a woman in my single-mothers-by-chance support group admit that she intentionally got pregnant in this way. But the head of the New York–based Single Mothers by Choice organization, Jane Mattes, indicated that she hears of this plan often. The frightening reality is that Jane and her organization seem to condone intentional pregnancy with an unsuspecting partner. In Mattes's book, *Single Mothers by Choice*, the certified social worker advises how to keep Dad out of the picture. "Do not put anything in writing referring to his being the father, tell no one about his identity, do not give the child his last name, and do not put his name on the birth certificate . . ."

Some women are apparently unable to admit even to themselves that what they did was intentional. When one woman, Megan, became pregnant, she was dating a man who had no intentions of getting married or becoming a father. She was around 40 years old and registered on the rolls of adoption agencies, and she told me that she knew exactly when her period and ovulations occurred. She describes her pregnancy as "accidental."

mission in mind. "At 32, I ended a long-term relationship and decided at that time that 35 was the magic age to have a baby. At 34, I decided to have sex with someone in order to get pregnant."

In Wales, she went to a bar in search of the man who would father her child. She recalls telling a good friend, 'I'm going to get pregnant tonight.' And we laughed about it."

As the evening unfolded, Rachel met a Scottish guy. "He was really cute. I went to his house and we had sex all night. I don't think he had a clue as to what was going on; I don't think he had ever met an American woman like me. But he should have wondered when he brought out a condom and I just sort of tossed it up onto the dresser."

In this case, the casual contact and the wild sex didn't result in a pregnancy. A year later, Rachel is grateful. "I'm so glad it didn't happen that way." She's now the mother of a newborn she conceived through artificial insemination. "It was so simple and safe this way."

Then there is the adoptive mother who told me about a friend who realized that her long-term relationship with a man was ending. A carefully timed love-making session was planned, not to keep his interest but to get pregnant. "She turned around and filed for child support. Why not? He could have prevented the relations," she argued. True, but her methods were still grossly dishonest. Who could possibly advocate this route to motherhood?

At worst, this practice of using men can be downright deadly, carrying with it the possibility of HIV transmission from a stranger; at best it is fraudulent and can certainly strain a relationship.

But additionally, it's a deception that you, if you participate in such a scheme, will have to live with. Only you know
your intentions. I know that I would not want to live with this
burden of guilt. If you are seriously considering this route, you
may want to seek counseling.

Down the Road

Artificial insemination brings a few unique challenges that
you must deal with as time goes by. You will have to prepare
for your child's questions about his conception, as well as for
the possibility that he will want to pursue his donor father's
identity. Prepare your child with a healthy attitude about his
conception, stressing that you wanted him very much and love
him very much, and give him access to absolutely all of the
donor information you can provide in order to guard against
the possibility of inbreeding.

TALKING TO YOUR CHILD ABOUT HIS CONCEPTION

In fact, explanations related to conception concern most
single mothers less than those related to the lack of a daddy.
The talk Mary plans for her son goes something like this: "I
wanted you very, very much. You were conceived differently
from most people." Here, she will give an explanation of the
typical conception and birth. "A wonderful man helped me to
have you by giving me his seed."

Elaine R. Gordon, Ph.D., author of *Mommy, Did I Grow
in Your Tummy?*, recommends disclosing whatever method

you've used to conceive your family. "You need to normal-ize the situation. In doing so, you can say, `Families are comprised of all sorts of configurations. Even though most families have the mommy and the daddy, there's no one right way to form a family.'"

Perhaps the most difficult question for single mothers con-cerning donor insemination is whether to describe the donor as the child's father. Lauren, the Episcopalian priest with the seven-year-old daughter, will not. "I do not feel that the suc-cessful donor is the father of my child. My child does not have a father; she had a genetic package."

Karen does view the donor as the biological father but tells her three-year-old son, Daniel, that "he has nothing to do with our lives other than helping me to have you." When Daniel asked "Where's my daddy?" out of the blue one day, Karen responded, "Mommy's not married right now. When I get mar-ried we'll have one."

Everyone has hopes and dreams for the perfect future and family down the road, but do be careful not to set your child up with false expectations regarding a father. Don't lead your child to believe that he will definitely have a father one day; instead, say something like, "I hope someday you'll have a father, and who knows, that could happen, if I marry." It's a simple matter of picking your words carefully. We don't know for certain what the future will bring.

Because artificial insemination is not an everyday occur-rence, Gordon notes, "we don't yet have the terminology and the vocabulary to make it easily understood by a child. She sug-gests saying something like "He's not your everyday or live-in father, but he is your biological father."

"I'm aware of the agony that goes along with not knowing who your father is," says Linda, "and I would have to be an idiot to think that my daughter wouldn't be the least bit curious." On the other hand, she points out that every child in the world has a handicap of some kind. Linda plans to talk about the issue honestly and emphasize the fact to her daughter that she doesn't *know* who her Daddy is. "I want her to know that I don't have the information. It's not hidden in the recesses of my mind."

Through role play, you can prepare your child with a response for classmates and friends when asked a question about his father.

Dr. Hanafin, the Beverly Hills psychologist, recommends developing a support network of women who've had children through donor insemination, reading literature on this topic and writing a letter to your child explaining why and how you came to create him in this unique way. The letter ensures that if anything were to happen to you, your child would still have access to his personal history.

WANTING TO MEET A DONOR DADDY

Depending on your contract, meeting a donor father might be a fairly simple matter of detective work or it might necessitate breaking the law.

Psychologist Paul J. Cibrowski, of Long Island University, is conducting a 10-year study of children of single mothers by choice. The study, which began in 1990, has revealed some interesting preliminary results.

Between four and seven years old, "children definitely do miss having a father," says Dr. Cibrowski. "This was the case whether it was boys or girls. One six-year-old boy told his mom, for instance, `I'd like my daddy to put me to bed and kiss me good-night.'"

Some have developed coping mechanisms. "One boy would call his grandfather 'Dad'; another, his uncle. Others use fantasy and say that their father travels a lot or is a policeman or a pilot and that's why he's not around."

Children seven to nine responded to questions about a father by declaring, "I don't have a father." One girl experienced "a certain wistfulness with regard to her father," notes Cibrowski. "She wondered about him and what type of person he was."

Count on having your child express an interest in his donor father. It is natural, and no matter how much you might pray for it not to happen, you will be unable to will the child's desire away. Remain calm and share all that you know about his or her donor father: the sports he liked, for example, or his height or eye color. Paint a picture of the man who helped you conceive your child.

Lauren, the priest, takes a rather extreme stance on the subject of a possible meeting. She doesn't believe the interest in a man who hasn't been around is natural or warranted. Instead, she feels that her daughter needs to realize that "this is the hand she's been dealt. All this stuff about people tracking down their roots is nonsense. I have no sympathy for these spoiled-brat adopted kids who are tracking down people who left them. It destroys trust. It sets up a false standard for parenthood."

In Lauren's mind, "it's the person who gets up at three A.M. because the child is throwing up, the person who sews the button on 30 minutes before the bus arrives who is the parent." When Eve was about six, she went through a spell of being upset about not having a father, says Lauren. "It was when she became aware that everyone is supposed to have one."

Lauren handled the situation by saying, "This is the way that you were born; this is the only way that I could have you. Are you happy you were born? Are you glad you're here? Because it wouldn't have worked any other way. Any other way it wouldn't have been you."

If the subject comes up again, Lauren says, she will be understanding and sympathetic. But ultimately, "she's just going to have to get over it."

At the other end of the spectrum is Linda, who told me, "I will work with every fiber of my being to create self-esteem that can't be shaken, but in the end, if Gretel decides she wants to find her anonymous donor father, I will do everything that I can to help her."

At some point, children of anonymous donors simply must be told that it is not possible to meet their donor fathers. Yet, my suspicion is that in the years to come, advocacy groups who challenge closed documents in court and who take illegal steps to obtain identifying information related to anonymous donors will be on the increase.

FEAR OF INBREEDING

Inbreeding is a fear commonly associated with artificial insemination. Sperm banks have pregnancy limits for donors—usually 10 pregnancies. Women who use the bank worry that down the road their children might date or marry a half-brother or -sister.

As long as you are open and honest with your child about his conception, he should harbor no shame. Any expressions of concern about a potential mate will be only natural.

When you talk about the birds and the bees with your child or when you believe your child may soon become sexually active, you'll want to be sure that he is armed with as much genetic information as possible and suggest that he talk with all lovers about this danger, as a precaution.

Future Trends: A Combination of Finding a Donor and Using a Bank

I believe that over time, studies will conclude that openness concerning donor insemination leads to healthier families. In striving to make donor insemination as healthy a route as possible for all concerned, single mothers need to arm themselves with as much personal information as possible about the donor fathers of their children. They also need to make this information available to their children.

My hope is that in the future, recruiting donors through face-to-face contact will become the way most single women pursue insemination. In order to advertise for and recruit your own donor, you will need to assure the candidates that they will not be responsible for child support, probably their greatest concern. Your agreement should involve a legal contract.

Your own concern may revolve around your personal privacy and the fear that the donor may intrude into your life.

I have drawn up a plan for recruiting your own donor that takes into account all of the fears and passions of single mothers I've heard, the yearnings of adopted children and those I believe will surface in children of anonymous donors, as well as the information I wish I had to pass along to my own daughter. In my opinion, it's a much healthier route to single motherhood.

Some women may be uncomfortable approaching potential donors. For them, an advertisement for a personal donor in a local newspaper is a good option. It might read something like this:

"IN SEARCH OF: Male, Caucasian, Christian, six feet tall to six foot two, age 21 to 34. College-educated, athletic. To donate sperm in exchange for generous monetary compensation. Contractual agreement. Must be willing to be identified and possibly approached after the child reaches his eighteenth birthday. Call Jennifer: (202) 222-1234."

Determine the going rate that sperm banks in your area pay donors. If they pay $40 a specimen, you might consider offering $75. The beauty of this route is that you can contractually stipulate that the donor not have been instrumental in the pregnancies of 10 other women, the cap on pregnancies per donor within most sperm banks. There is never a guarantee, of course, but this plan may alleviate the possibility of a donor's lacking interest in his child because he's already been approached by nine other offspring.

During your interviews:

- Ask to see photos of the potential donor's family.

- Ask a potential donor how he thinks he will feel if he is approached by your child 18 years down the road.

- Stress the importance of a positive meeting with your child in the future if your child desires an encounter. Emphasize that his behavior in that one meeting could affect another individual's mental health and emotional well-being for a very long time.

- Assure potential donors that neither you nor your child will be entitled to information concerning his identity until the child reaches the age of majority (18 or 21).

- Assure potential donors that the contractual agreement you sign will not allow for you to file for child support.

- Encourage him to run the contract by a lawyer if necessary; perhaps even volunteer to pay the legal costs.

After you select a potential donor:

- Remain on a first-name basis with him.

- Consult with a sperm bank about the donor you have found. Plan to have him tested in the same manner as any other donor.

- Have your donor fill out a medical questionnaire from a sperm bank.

- Negotiate a deal with a sperm bank in which you can use their contracts, and have their tests administered on your donor's specimen. At the very least, use the bank's contracts as stepping-off points.

- Consult with a lawyer who is well-versed in contracts, reproductive assistance legislation and family law in your jurisdiction.

- Don't ask the donor to reveal his last name or social security number and permanent address to you, but do require that he exchange identifying information with your lawyer or sperm bank to ensure confidentiality and openness.

- Ask your donor for photographs of him that you may keep in order to show your child before he turns 18 if and when he inquires about his biological father.

- Try to find out a few personal things about your donor that will help your child develop a concrete image of the man who helped him to be, as well as provide him with tidbits that he might be interested in knowing about his biological father. Find out such things as whether he was president of the glee club or first chair clarinet in high school. Did he date the homecoming queen? Ask him about sports and pets: Did he grow up with St. Bernards?

- Explain to your donor that you cannot guarantee that your child will want to seek him out. The information and photos that you are able to supply may satiate your child's interest, but if not, at least this way you will be at peace knowing you've given him the option of finding out more.

If you're ready to proceed, locate a bank that will work with you and the donor you bring in yourself. Most banks will

offer your donor a medical questionnaire and have the specimen screened and quarantined as they do with their own
donors. Enlist the help of a physician when the screening
results are back and when you are ready to proceed with the
insemination.

SEVEN

Adoption: Yet Another Option

Judy, a nurse, subscribed to the belief that she would "work a while, get married and have a family." As it turned out, she worked for a while, got married, worked some more, and some more. Eventually, she got divorced. "Parenting had a way of getting out of my to-do list," she declared.

But before she got divorced, she and her husband suffered a couple of miscarriages and explored adoption. Even on her own, Judy carried with her that strong desire for a "snuggly little person to cuddle with."

A First Choice for Many

Before filling the loneliness in her life with a daughter from India, Judy, realizing she didn't need to bear a child to love one, filled out mountains of paperwork and articulated her innermost yearnings to a social worker. Other women seeking to adopt run advertisements in newspapers, and at times confront language, cultural and socioeconomic barriers—all for the opportunity to share their lives with a little one.

Spared the stretch marks and the C-section scars of pregnancy and childbirth, but not necessarily the emotional highs and lows, some adoptive moms first lay eyes on their children in overcrowded orphanages, bustling airport terminals and county courthouses. And while there's a common assumption that this route is only a last resort for the woman who discovers she cannot conceive, many adoptive mothers have harbored aspirations to adopt for as long as they can remember.

With the realization that she loved children but was tired of caring for everyone else's through such things as baby-sitting arrangements and Girl Scout activities, Joyce, a 40-year-old administrator, set her sights on adoption so she could nurture her own. "The experience of carrying a baby was not an issue with me," declared Joyce, who never even gave artificial insemination or a relationship without strings a second thought. "Because of my personal makeup, I could not go out and intentionally get pregnant. If I was going to go through a pregnancy, I wanted a husband. I did not want to bring a child into the world and say, `You don't have a father.'"

Adoption is often the first choice of other single women for similar reasons, says Barbara Marshall, co-chairperson of Washington, D.C.'s Association of Single Adoptive Parents. The majority of these women are in their late thirties and forties and college-educated, says Marshall. They typically "reach a point where they're not doing things the way they were supposed to do them... They're not married, and they come to the realization that if they want children, they will have to do it on their own."

Marshall believes there is still a social stigma attached to pregnancy for single women—a stigma they avoid by adopting. She believes this stigma is the main reason single women choose adoption as a route to motherhood. Additionally, they circumvent such maternity problems as nausea, hospital costs, bed rest and fatigue.

A few women are drawn to adoption by the idea of rescuing a child or offering him a solid chance at life. When talk-show hostess Oprah Winfrey announced her desire to adopt, she told the *National Examiner*, "Having a child come from my body isn't as important to me as being able to change the life of a child."

Some women do fall back on adoption only after they learn they are unable to conceive or carry a child. "My first choice was to have my own physical child," says Leigh, a 48-year-old attorney in California. But after going through several inseminations and taking the fertility drug Chlomid, which led to the discovery of ovarian cysts and other complications, she concluded that "it was not meant to be." Leigh ended up adopting five-year-old Valerie and soon hopes to adopt a toddler.

Emotional Factors to Consider About Adoption

Adoption carries its own unique set of challenges, and single women encounter a few additional hurdles. It's a competitive venture, and couples under 40 are often viewed as the most desirable parents. Therefore, a bit more flexibility and open-mindedness with regard to a type of child may be necessary for a single mother. That is not to say that you won't be able to find a healthy white newborn—in this chapter we'll introduce you to a single woman who did. The fact is, most adoptive parents hope to adopt white infants, and as a result, the odds are extremely competitive. You will increase your chances of success if you are flexible, patient and persistent.

To determine your flexibility, you will need to ask yourself some serious questions—questions about the race, age and sex of your adopted child. Do you have a fixed image in your mind? And could these expectations affect the degree of love that you are able to give a child? Is it important to you that your child resemble you physically? An older child of mixed race or of a background other than Caucasian is much easier to adopt than a healthy Caucasian infant. Expanding your concept of the type of child you would accept will increase your chances for adoption.

Patience and devotion, at times more than nine months' worth, are necessary to succeed within the adoption circuit. Leigh, the California attorney, followed a four-year-old girl around a small room with glass windows, trying to strike up conversation, without much success. County social workers looked on as the youngster, then a ward of the court, went over to a chest of drawers and proceeded to pull everything out onto the floor. Because of her behavior, the social workers wrote off that initial meeting as a disaster. But while the hour-long struggle to connect with Valerie "seemed like forever" to Leigh, it was not the last time she would come calling on Valerie in her search for a child to adopt. It is not uncommon for the process of adoption to take a single mother up to two years, from filling out application forms to tucking a youngster in at night.

Ideal candidates for adoption are homeowners who are less than 40 years old and thriving financially. Because there are so many families looking to adopt, birth mothers and agencies can afford to be choosy. A lifestyle suitable for child-rearing and an income that can offer a child economic advantages earn points with those picking parents.

Luck and preparedness also have a great deal to do with a single mother's success in adoption. With experience in adoption law and therefore some insight into the mind-set of young birth mothers, Nancie Quick, an attorney in Charleston, South Carolina, geared up for adoption by setting personal and professional goals to make herself more attractive to the young women who would choose families for their children. And it paid off; she is now the mother of a 17-month-old curly-headed blue-eyed boy named William. Nancie's goals were to:

1. Get completely out of debt.

2. Buy a new car and have it completely paid for.

3. Buy more disability and life insurance.

4. Land a secure job with benefits, paid holidays and sick days.

Any single woman planning to adopt should consider making a similar plan. You may want to substitute a new house for the new-car goal. Being prepared is a large part of the battle.

You may be able to ease the cost of adoption through your company's benefits package if it includes an adoption assistance program. For instance, *The Washington Post's* plan will reimburse 50 percent of all eligible adoption expenses up to a maximum of $5,000. Eligible expenses include public and properly authorized private-agency placement fees, application and registration fees, court costs, lawyers' fees and other legal fees, temporary foster care charges, transportation costs for the child and maternity expenses for the birth mother. The plan, however, will not cover voluntary donations, or contributions and fees related to legal guardianship.

Nearly all adoptions require a home study or some type of investigation, though specifics vary from state to state. Catholic Charities, a United Way agency, is just one organization licensed to perform home studies. Each state has minimum standards that homes must meet. The home study involves interviews, during which a social worker asks about such things as the prospective parent's health status, employment history and marital status, as well as more personal information related to religious views, upbringing and values. Reasons for wanting to adopt are also discussed.

During this process, which a few would-be parents liken to an interrogation, you may be tempted to gloss over the truth in order to come across as a better candidate. Leigh had a strong urge to hide her history of breast cancer and the fact that she was a victim of incest. "But I decided going into this that nothing in my history was a negative against me personally. It was something that had happened to me." By being up-front and honest with the social worker, Leigh was able to assure her that she had been through therapy and successfully dealt with the issues. Nine months later, she had an extra mouth to feed and an extra head of hair with honey-colored highlights to style. Leigh reflects back on the home study and sees it as a "valuable, healing experience."

Another consideration with regard to adoption is that the health of an infant cannot be guaranteed unless you closely monitor the pregnancy of the birth mother whose child you hope to adopt. In fact, the entire process can be downright mysterious.

But mystery and dreaming can also be part of the intrigue. When Joyce flew to New York's LaGuardia airport to meet her new daughter, who would arrive by plane from India, she wasn't sure what height or weight her adopted two-year-old might be; in fact her office had a betting pool as to the toddler's vital statistics. But when the plane touched ground, Joyce was prepared with five outfits, running the gamut in sizes from 18 months to 4T.

Types of Adoptions

If you are comfortable with the emotional challenges of adoption and are ready to further explore the route to motherhood, you will want to become familiar with the four categories of adoptions and the factors that distinguish one from another (these categories are not necessarily mutually exclusive): private, agency, international or foreign, and special-needs adoptions.

A private, or independent, adoption involves a face-to-face meeting between a birth mother and a prospective adoptive mother. The two usually connect via a newspaper ad or a mutual acquaintance. Lawyers are hired to relinquish birth parents' rights and to give an adoptive mother sole custody.

An agency adoption may be private and run by a nonprofit corporation or sponsored by a church group; the agency acts as the liaison between birth parents and adoptive parents. Public agencies are often run through county welfare departments. In order to adopt through an agency, you will meet with a social worker, fill out an application and, if accepted, have your name added to a waiting list of other prospective parents.

International, or foreign adoptions involve children from other countries who have been often orphaned or abandoned. Most single women use U.S. agencies that specialize in overseas adoptions.

Special-needs adoptions involve children of mixed race or difficult family backgrounds that may include neglect or abuse. Other children in this arena have physical or mental handicaps, such as learning disabilities or mental retardation.

Families Adopting Children Everywhere (FACE), a national public-service organization based in Baltimore, sponsors conferences and a one-week course, "Family Building Through Adoptions," for $90 in the mid-Atlantic region. Single-parent adoption organizations and support groups are also a wonderful source of information.

Finding an Adoption that Suits Your Needs

Circumstances such as your age, salary and health, as well as limits you impose on the expenditures of money, energy, emotional risk and time, will affect your decision as to which type of adoption is best for you.

Consultations with agencies, adoption attorneys and other single adoptive mothers found through support groups and associations can help you get a clearer sense of your options.

Private adoptions carry a tremendous amount of risk. Interviews with birth parents can drag on, a mother's decision may be withheld for a period after the baby's birth, and expenses can mount up. Emotional and financial investments can run high. Despite your being courted as a serious candidate, and even after being selected, you have no guarantee that you will parent the infant. Cases of birth mothers who have promised their infant to multiple couples, bilking all of them out of money and living off them in high style, have made many adoptive parents wary of such direct dealings. Depending on state legislation, private adoptions may include expenses related to lawyers, the birth mother's hospital bills and sometimes even her living and loss-of-income expenses, and may run as high as $15,000 to $20,000.

Being at the right place at the right time has a lot to do with success in private adoptions; single mothers have had their share of victories. That was the case for Elizabeth, whose meeting with her son's birth mother, Polly, came through a personal introduction from a teenage friend. The birth mother of Elizabeth's son was initially re-ferred to her as a client.

But from the very first phone conversation with Polly, "something clicked," says Elizabeth, an attorney. "She told me she was looking for an adoptive family and she wanted someone creative; I was a former ballet teacher. She said she wanted someone with a Presbyterian or Episcopalian background; I had been an Episcopalian for the last 10 years."

Elizabeth believes that Polly's childhood background greatly influenced her choice of a family for her son Kenneth. "Her father left when she was four; her mother had no job skills and therefore no job or money. Polly's concern was not that I was a married mother but rather that I was stable and secure," she noted.

Elizabeth's adoption of Kenneth was extremely open. Polly had a key to her house, a key to her car. They shopped for nursery furniture, opened baby shower presents and went to Lamaze class together. Elizabeth was also Polly's birthing coach. But before the documents were signed, Polly and her son's father did ask Elizabeth to make them a few promises regarding their son:

1. Kenneth's child care would not be through a corporate child-care center. Instead, he should have a day nanny until at least age two.

2. Kenneth would be raised Presbyterian or Episcopalian.

3. Kenneth was not to be allowed to play football; instead, he would be encouraged to play soccer. (Polly considered football to be "neanderthal," and her son's father had injured both knees playing the game.)

4. Kenneth would grow up with a cat in the house. (Polly loved cats.)

If you are dealing directly with the mother, you should expect to fulfill some promises, and be ready to extend an offer if no requests are made.

In domestic adoptions, "there are far fewer opportunities for single parents for healthy infants," notes Clyde

Tolley, executive director of Families Adopting Children Everywhere, "but they do occur through word-of-mouth or advertising." Quick, a Charleston, S.C., lawyer with experience in adoption law, agrees. "There are 20 families for every child up for adoption in an agency," she points out. And at any given time, between 16 and 18 families are on the waiting list for children through Catholic Charities, an adoption agency operated by the Arlington Diocese in Virginia.

Some agencies have age and marital restrictions that disqualify some prospective parents. You may not make it onto the rolls if you are over 40 or single. "To young girls who place their children through adoption, if you're over 40, you seem ancient," says Quick, who has helped many of these young birth mothers find families for their babies.

When Betsy called agencies listed in the Yellow Pages, she was able to find one that would work with single parents. But in order to qualify as an adoptive parent, she was informed that she would have to quit her job and stay with the child for three years. Few single people can afford that luxury. Most of us would quickly reach Betsy's conclusion: "I don't think they *really* wanted single parents."

Other women with similar experiences decide to pursue international or biracial adoptions where fewer restrictions apply. Judy, the divorced woman, started searching for an agency that specialized in international adoptions when she realized that babies placed through the county welfare agencies rarely went home with single people. "They had a list up the kazoo for married parents," she declared. "I didn't want to take in a 13-year-old girl who's about to leave home. That would not be the right timing for me."

For Nina, the risk involved with a private adoption was too great. "If the birth mother changes her mind, it can be likened to a miscarriage," she declared. Nina could not face the possibility of a private adoption falling through; so she decided to sign up with a U.S. agency that specialized in international adoptions. "Once I made the decision to adopt, I wanted to know that I would have a child. I wanted more of a guarantee. If one agency source fell through, there would be another. I wouldn't be back at the drawing board."

Single mothers leery of their ability to find a child through adoption will find that their chances improve when they go through an agency that handles international adoptions. The International Families Agency in Washington, D.C., has helped approximately 100 single women adopt from foreign countries in the past six years. Its director, Mrudula Rao, has found the best bets for them to be infants and children from China, India and South America. Other agencies have successfully helped single women adopt children from Russia and Eastern Europe. International adoptions are relatively low-risk with a reputable agency. You should plan to pay about $7,000 to $15,000. That amount covers the costs of foster care, the orphanage, a passport, air fares and possibly a travel escort.

Judy zoomed in on an international adoption because it was a route that allowed her to get a younger child. "I wanted a snuggly little person to cuddle—diapers, bottles—the whole bit," Judy chirped, adding, "That's how you have children. You have infants and they grow up. It never occurred to me to adopt a school-aged child."

After going to an informational meeting with the International Families Agency, Joyce learned that Latin

America, Asia and India were all good possibilities for single-parent adoptions. She leaned toward a child from India because the culture appealed to her. "I found them to be very gentle and bright people." Just 10 months later, she would meet her daughter, Sarah, one week shy of her second birthday.

As for the most active areas for single-parent adoptions, Tolley notes that "Eastern Europe is hot right now." Other areas that have an open door for single parents are China and Vietnam. Tolley predicts that because Vietnam does not require a parent to spend time in the country before adopting a child, it will become even more popular over the next few years for single parents. It's an option that can cut down significantly on the expense of international adoptions.

County or state welfare systems offer women seeking to adopt a child one of the least expensive methods. Children obtained through low-budget adoptions often offer special challenges to a single mother. Leigh spent only $2,000—a typical sum—by going through the county court system and taking care of her own legal paperwork. The total included an adoptive-parent training course, a home study, follow-up counseling services and ultimately, the privilege of parenting Valerie.

Leigh did not believe that her strength was in handling a smaller child. In fact, she felt strongly that she wanted an older child. "I wanted one with whom I could communicate; I wanted one who talked."

In moving toward that goal, Leigh explored the children in the hands of the local courts and signed up for a program in Sacramento called Fost-adopt. The program licenses foster parents, who in many cases can get a child more quickly than they would through adoption; but there's also a risk because the rights of the child's parents are not yet entirely terminated, and the foster parents may lose the child after they've become attached.

Leigh also signed up for a class made up of about four families who were going to adopt. During the six-week program, the group role-played to familiarize themselves with issues related to adoptions of older children. They explored common misconceptions of parents going into adoptions of children with special needs or from troubled backgrounds—for instance, that the child's response to being welcomed into your home will be one of unqualified gratitude.

The group explored such scenarios as, What would you do if you were in a store and caught your child shoplifting? As Leigh learned in the course, "that may have been a means of survival for the child."

Adoptions of older or special-needs children "are not for everyone," notes Tolley. "Because these children are coming from backgrounds of abuse, neglect and exposure to drugs, parents very definitely need the proper preparation." But for those who take on the challenge of these adoptions, the satisfaction is immense. Leigh is so delighted with four-year-old Valerie that she plans to return to the same adoption arena soon for a toddler.

Magical, Memorable Meetings

Rrrrrrrriiiiinnnnnng! After the phone call finally comes, alerting you to a possible match, it isn't unusual to have to be scraped from the ceiling. With just a few more signatures and days remaining between the long-awaited meeting of mother and child, most women enlist friends to help them pack for overseas trips or stage a warm welcome.

Because Joyce didn't speak her adopted daughter's language, she brought a little terry-cloth doll to the airport to help convey her love and commitment when she first met her two-year-old daughter. "I wanted to hug the doll and then hug her," explained Joyce, who had a harried 20 minutes to sign papers, grab her daughter's passport and make a mad dash to the shuttle that would take them to the next terminal where they would catch another flight home. "I just kept saying in what little Indian I knew, `I love you, I love you, I love you.'"

The doll had absolutely no impact on her daughter, recalls Joyce. "She was scared." Like many children who are adopted through international agencies and orphanages, she arrived with lice and smelled horrendous. "The first thing she did was pee on me; she had no underwear on." After a makeshift cleanup in an airport restroom, the two caught a flight to Washington, D.C. It was while sitting in the airplane side-by-side that a real connection was made with little Sarah. "I had polished my nails the night before; hers had little bits of polish on them. She looked at hers, then at mine. That's what clicked."

When the time came for Polly, a young birth mother, to part with her two-day-old son in the hospital, it was extremely emotional and difficult for both her and the adoptive mother, Elizabeth, in spite of their love and respect for one another. Recalls Elizabeth, "She had to ring a bell when she was ready. It was much harder for her to give him up than she thought it would be. When they physically came and took him away, out of her arms, she wouldn't let me go back in the room. It was the hardest thing. I don't want anybody to think it was easy. I wished at that point that we could both have him, but of course I knew that was impossible."

Elizabeth reflected once again on the birth mother's circumstances. "She didn't have a job. She didn't have a family that would support her. What would become of them? They would end up in a family shelter. But still, that was really very, very hard. I wanted him so bad-ly and I wanted to take him home, but I hurt so much for her. It was bittersweet."

Judy likens the initial meeting with her nine-month-old daughter from India to the first few hours and days after labor and delivery. "You just stare and snuggle. We looked at each other for days."

Those moments were also a playful period for Judy and her daughter, Mary. "We zipped and unzipped jackets and counted fingers. It was a 'let's get acquainted' kind of time—a 'hi, let's explore' period."

When the plane carrying Joyce and Sarah touched down at National Airport in Washington, D.C., a black limousine with a car seat and several chilled bottles of sparkling cider was waiting. About 25 people were there to greet the pair. A few of the friends, many of them adoptive families as well, piled in the limousine to join Joyce and Sarah for the ride back to Sarah's new home to celebrate.

Back Home

After the party, Joyce led Sarah into her new bedroom, done up with white IKEA furniture, yellow curtains and a bright pink bedspread. The feminine decor "meant nothing to her," recalls Joyce. After putting the exhausted toddler to bed, Joyce went to sleep on the floor beside her. "I didn't want her to wake up and be afraid."

Four-year-old Valerie's homecoming was more subdued when Leigh brought her back to her California housing complex. Valerie had previously been to the suburban home and even spent the night, but "she was tight and rigid, guarded and scared," recalled Leigh. When she came for good, she brought along all her worldly possessions—a garbage bag half filled with clothes and a couple of toys.

When it finally dawned on Valerie, who was taken away from her parents during a police raid in California, that she was at Leigh's to stay, she experienced a period of mourning. In spite of the somewhat chaotic and nomadic lifestyle from which she came, Valerie would often reveal that she missed her parents, notes Leigh. "Initially, it was really painful for me. But I wouldn't try to minimize it. I would just acknowledge her feelings. I figured she had a right to those feelings, even though I was angry at her parents for treating her like she wasn't important."

A poignant recollection of the last time she saw her birth mother is etched in Valerie's mind. It was during the raid. As she told Leigh and even reported to her classmates, "She reached up to get donuts. She handed them to me and told me to feed myself and my brothers and sisters." Notes Leigh, "Valerie says they ate a lot of donuts."

While blessed with children who may be able to sleep through the night, adoptive parents of older children can't, of course, expect instant gratification and love. Because of abusive and neglectful backgrounds, many of these children are forlorn, distrustful, or filled with rage. In the beginning, Leigh found that daily discipline problems were a fact of life. "Valerie would wake up being oppositional, cry if I told her to come down to breakfast, not want the cereal, have problems with playmates and throw tantrums."

Valerie's ability to show and give love ran a similarly chaotic course. At first, "she wouldn't show love at all," noted Leigh. Then she would receive it but only show it in a guarded way. Now she is showing who she is. "She has blossomed. She has gotten very bonded to me and totally changed my life. I believe in part that is because it's just the two of us."

Down the Road

Most adoptive parents realize the importance of honesty with regard to their child's adoption. The impact of this openness varies with each child. Tolley spoke of families he's known in which there were several adopted children, each with different reactions to his history. "One child may develop an intense interest in his homeland as he gets older, whereas a brother or a sister could care less."

Just remember, "you can't make them get interested in their background, and you can't prevent them from being interested," Tolley says. But you can set limits. A nine-year-old who expresses an intense interest in returning to Colombia, for instance, might be told, "Gee, that's okay to want to visit Colombia; but I think that you should wait until you're 18."

The subject of birth parents may be approached at a very earlyage if your child's skin tone is noticeably different from yours. Says Joyce of her four-year-old daughter from India, "She knows that she needed a mommy and I wanted a little girl. She knows that the woman's tummy she grew in has beautiful brown skin like hers. We look at pictures of women in India."

Take a supportive stance with regard to your child's interest in his adoptive history, advises Tolley. Try to answer your child's questions in a positive and age-appropriate manner. Judy spoke to her daughter about her loneliness before she came along. "I talk about when I first saw her and how happy I was when we snuggled."

Some personal circumstances surrounding the adoption of a child, such as the child's abandonment, are better left unsaid, or at the very least, carefully phrased. In spite of a child's very natural interest in his birth parents, there is no need to "compromise the status of your family," says Tolley. "It doesn't have to mean that you want to have the birth parents over for dinner every night."

In many cases, children who are adopted through international orphanages come with no parental records. At an orphanage in India, Joyce tried to find out information about the birth parents of her two-year-old daughter. "They don't keep records; there are no birth certificates," Joyce pointed out. "It's impossible." Tolley believes that such is the norm for international adoptions.

With the little information regarding the background of her child, Joyce plans to focus on the facts she does have. "I have her birth date. I know that her birth mother was young and that she got along well with the other residents. When we look at pictures of Indian women, I can tell her that her mother was probably very beautiful, because she's so beautiful."

All adopted children will face the issue of separation and loss, notes Tolley, even if they have no recollection of their birth parents. "They will wonder, `What happened?' and `Why wasn't I wanted?'"

If, in spite of your positive and supportive conversations, your child seems to still be struggling with the issue of his or her genetic heritage, you should be prepared to share all of the records you have surrounding the adoption and refer him to a counselor or to an adoptee support group.

It's All Worth It

Many an adoptive mother has tiptoed into the nursery to see her child's face lit only by a soft night-light. Most, like Elizabeth, still feel "very awed, amazed and thankful" to have their children. "Polly gave me the greatest gift anybody could give me," she concludes.

Judy, the nurse who divorced, reflects back on her life before motherhood. "I remember being quite lonely, wondering what I was going to do with my time. I filled it with a child. It brought me warmth, love, companionship and family life."

Few rewards could be more gratifying than the aspiration that Valerie recently confided to her adoptive mother, Leigh. "She tells me that she wants to grow up and be an adoptive mom."

A Final Thought

You Have Just Begun....

I have good news. Single motherhood, whether it comes about by chance or by choice, can be a rewarding journey for you and provide a healthy, happy and thriving environment for your child.

If you became pregnant by chance, single motherhood can give you confidence that you can make it through difficult waters and emerge a more capable, giving and compassionate person. If by choice, taking this less traditional route can intensify your appreciation of parenthood. Regardless of how you got there, however, single motherhood helps you grow.

But the most important aspect of single motherhood is not what it does to or for us; it's how it affects our children and what we can do to better their lives.

This book tackles the issues unique to motherhood that begins with a single woman. Certain fundamental responsibilities—paternity tests, child support, custody and visitation agreements, financial and psychological health, providing explanations about a donor father—must be addressed early in your infant's development.

But after two years spent talking and listening to women who embarked on motherhood without a steadfast partner, I am convinced that the most critical actions relate to the handling of biological family members—be they estranged fathers, genetic donors or birth parents who placed their child through an adoption agency. If handled improperly, these actions and conversations can be detrimental to your child's well-being and even leave permanent scars. Loving your child is not necessarily enough. You must think long-term.

Once you've dealt with those issues exclusive to unmarried mothers you will need to keep researching and reading. There are hundreds of volumes on the practical aspects of single parenting and specialty books that address such skills as time management, easy, quick, and inexpensive meal planning and disciplinary techniques, which can make the journey easier and more fun. You can also take cues from surveys and articles that highlight factors prevalent in healthy families regardless of configuration.

Finally, recognize your limits and your strengths. Strive to make your legacy one that includes your child's affirmation: "I may not have a dad, but I have the best mom I could ever imagine."

RESOURCES

ADOPTION

Committee for Single Adoptive Parents
P.O. Box 15084
Chevy Chase, MD 20815
(202) 966-6367
Offers information and source lists for prospective and actual adoptive parents.

Association of Single Adoptive Parents
(703) 521-0632
A support group for single adoptive parents and those considering adoption. Offers a newsletter, meetings and presentations by professionals concerning adoption and child development, as well as social activities. Membership is $20.

Families Adopting Children Everywhere (FACE)
P.O. Box 28058
Baltimore, MD 21237
(410) 488-2656
Annual conferences and courses. For specific dates call (410) 488-2656.

HOMOSEXUAL PARENTING

Gay and Lesbian Parents Coalition, International (GLPCI)
Box 50360
Washington, D.C. 20091
(202) 583-8029
A membership organization that offers support, a bibliography of books for children of lesbian and gay parents and guides for coming out to your children. Membership is $15 per year.

INFERTILITY

Resolve, Inc.
1310 Broadway, Department G
Sumerville, MA 02144-1733
(617) 643-2424
A national organization to help those dealing with infertility. Local chapter meetings offer counseling and support. For more information, send a self-addressed, stamped envelope.

SINGLE MOTHERHOOD

Single Mother
P.O. Box 68
Midland, NC 28107
(704) 888-KIDS
Offers how-to information for single mothers and helps make connections with local self-help and support groups. Publishes *Single Mother* magazine.

Single Mothers by Choice (SMC)
P.O. Box 1642
Gracie Square Station
New York, NY 10028
(212) 988-0993
A membership organization, $40 for those outside of New York; $60 for New York residents, which includes membership in an ongoing "Tryers" group and monthly meetings. The organization provides names of single mothers in various states and, for an additional cost, copies of previously published newspaper and magazine articles related to single motherhood. Offers meetings in New York for "thinkers," those debating whether or not to pursue single motherhood.

SUGGESTED READING

ADOPTION

Schaffer, Judith, and Christina Lindstrom, *How to Raise an Adopted Child*. New York: Crown Publishers, Inc., 1989. Sensitively written by the cofounders and codirectors of the Manhattan-based Center for Adoptive Families, this book thoughtfully tackles the questions and issues that most adoptive parents will face.

ANGER

Smedes, Lewis B., *Forgive and Forget: Healing the Hurts We Don't Deserve*. San Francisco: Harper San Francisco, 1991. A comforting book that, for the sake of your own happiness, shows you how to move from hurting and hating to healing and forgiveness.

DISCIPLINE AND PARENTING SKILLS

Dobson, James. *Dare to Discipline*. Wheaton, Ill.: Tyndale House Publishers, 1970. This classic includes a chapter on teaching respect and responsibility to children, examples of discipline gone awry and basic rules that make discipline effective.

Leman, Kevin. *Making Children Mind without Losing Yours*. New York: Dell Publishing, 1984.

Nelson, Jane, Cheryl Erin, and Carol Delzer. *Positive Discipline for Single Parents*. Rocklin, Calif.: Prima Publishing, 1994. A practical guide to help singles parent on their own. Includes daily affirmations to build strength and combat feelings of isolation and loneliness.

Silberman, Mel. *Confident Parenting*. New York: Warner Books, 1988.

DONOR INSEMINATION

Noble, Elizabeth. *Having Your Baby by Donor Insemination: A Complete Resource Guide*. New York: Houghton Mifflin, 1987. A guidebook on the insemination process.

Baran, Annette, and Reuben Pananor. *Lethal Secrets: The Shocking Consequences and Unsolved Problems of Artificial Insemination*. New York: Warner Books, 1989. An exploration of the emotional impact of donor insemination on all the parties involved, from the donors to the recipients to the offspring.

American Fertility Society Patient Education Committee. "Guidelines for the Gamete Donation: 1993." Birmingham, Ala.: American Fertility Society, 1990. An informational booklet filled with procedures, precautions and definitions. Send your request with $3 to the American Fertility Society, 2140 11th Avenue South, Suite 200, Birmingham, AL 35205-2800.

FINANCIAL PLANNING

Berg, Adriane G. *Your Wealth-Building Years. Financial Planning for 18 to 36 Year-olds.* New York: New Market Press, 1991. An introductory book that provides and understanding of the importance of discipline, timing and planning and reviews basic investment strategies for a healthy and secure financial future.

FOR YOUR CHILD

Gordon, Elaine, Ph.D. *Mommy, Did I Grow in Your Tummy? Where Some Babies Come From.* Santa Monica, CA: Greenberg Press, 1993. This children's book tells the tale of a couple who used alternative reproduction to finally gain the child they so badly wanted.

GENERAL SINGLE PARENTING

Alexander, Shoshana. *In Praise of Single Parents: Mothers and Fathers Embracing the Challenge.* New York: Houghton Mifflin, 1994. An upbeat, realistic book featuring the sagas of single parents, both male and female, from all walks of life.

Mattes, Jane, C.S.W. *Single Mothers by Choice: A Guidebook for Single Women Who are Considering or Have Chosen Motherhood.* New York: Times Books, 1994. A very basic introduction for women seeking single motherhood.

LEGAL RIGHTS AND AGREEMENTS

Pekala, Beverly. *Don't Settle for Less: A Woman's Guide to Getting a Fair Divorce and Custody Settlement.* New York: Doubleday, 1992. A clear, insightful and honest tool written by a family law attorney to help women work their way through legal agreements concerning such things as custody and child support.

Ricci, Isolina. *Mom's House, Dad's House.* New York: MacMillan Publishing Co., 1982. A valuable handbook offering tactics for negotiation and sample agreements regarding support, visitation and custody.

SELF-ESTEEM

Felder, Leonard, Ph.D. *A Fresh Start: How to Let Go of Emotional Baggage and Enjoy Your Life Again..* New York: New American Library, 1987. Dr. Fedler suggests exercises and creative healing techniques to help people recognize and eliminate their harmful emotional baggage and move on to a positive new beginning, involving anything from relationships to personal success.

TIME MANAGEMENT

Douglass, Merrill E., and Donna Douglass. *Manage Your Time, Manage Your Work, Manage Yourself.* New York: AMACOM, 1993. Allow for more personal time or child-nurturing time by mastering time management. This book will tell you how to set priorities, streamline paperwork and balance your life.